GOD

GOD

WHAT IS HE LIKE?

Compiled
by
*William F.
Kerr*

Tyndale House Publishers, Inc. Wheaton, Illinois

Scripture quotations are from
the King James Version of the
Bible, unless otherwise designated.

Library of Congress
Catalog Card Number 77-77359
ISBN 0-8423-1098-3, paper
Copyright ©1977 by
Tyndale House Publishers, Inc.
Wheaton, Illinois. All rights reserved
First printing, June 1977
Printed in the United States of America

CONTENTS

Foreword

FOREWORD

Godly men of all ages have sensed the importance of the doctrine of God. And though admitting its vital place in maturing the Christian, yet they have hesitated to set forth the biblical teaching concerning it. Like Moses of old they realize that the ground which they traverse is "holy ground." Bible scholars have been reluctant to undertake such a daring project as to seek to deal with and make plain the biblical picture of God. But such reluctance has had to give way to duty.

The pressure of man's age-long desire to find the answer to the question: "What is God like?" has caused theologians to seek, to the best of their ability, to provide answers to that question.

It is for this reason that several faculty members from Western Conservative Baptist Seminary prepared a series of chapel messages dealing with the basic attributes and significant biblical characterizations of God. These lectures have been put into written form and now comprise the content of this book.

Some lectures have been further expanded; others remain essentially as they were delivered. In either case, very little editorial work has been done. Only brief additions or deletions have been made in order to bring about a unity of treatment and style.

Dr. Radmacher's chapter, "What Is God Like?" opens the study and sets the stage for the unfolding of the drama. Without an understandable answer to this question, there can be no genuine interest in God or his attributes. If God is so other-worldly or so far removed from man that only occasionally does he break into human history, then for man he has no true significance. Or if he is so identified with this world that he has no separate existence, then man sees himself as god. But such is not the biblical presentation of God, for as Dr. Radmacher answers: God is like Jesus Christ. He is a real God—both separate from the world and yet intensely interested in the world—and man can know him, worship him, fellowship with him, and, above all, do his will. He is the God and Father of our Lord Jesus Christ. For in Christ, he is fully revealed. ". . . the only begotten Son, which is in the bosom of the Father, he hath declared him" (John 1:18) and ". . . God, who commanded the light to shine out of darkness, hath shined in our hearts, to give the light of the knowledge of the glory of God in the face of Jesus Christ" (2 Corinthians 4:6). "To know God, study Jesus Christ," affirms Dr. Radmacher.

The subsequent chapters follow this same trend of thought as they seek to show forth God in all his majesty, glory, and grace. Enter, therefore, into the sacred precincts of the study of God as unfolded by these professors as they concur with the beloved Apostle John: "That which we have seen and heard declare we unto you, that ye also may have fellowship with us: and truly our fellowship is with the Father, and with his Son Jesus Christ" (1 John 1:3). As you do so, remember that this will be your eternal occupation in that celestial city which God is making ready for his own: "And I saw no temple therein: for the Lord God Almighty and the Lamb are the temple of it. And the city had no need of the sun, neither of the moon, to shine in it: for the glory of God did lighten it, and the Lamb is the light thereof . . . the throne of God and the Lamb shall be in it; and his servants shall serve him: And they shall see his face . . ." (Revelation 21:22, 23; 22:3, 4a).

To the glory of God and to the edification of his people, these lectures are prayerfully and humbly dedicated.

William F. Kerr, Editor

1

WHAT IS GOD LIKE?

Earl D. Radmacher
Th.D

Let us begin with a question: "How much can you trust a person?" Think about it for a moment. Your answer ultimately must be "as much as you know him." To the extent that you really know a person, to that same extent you are able to trust him. The same thing is true about God. It is good to know his promises and his program, but these are really meaningful only to the extent that you know his person. An unknown God can neither be trusted, served, nor worshiped. It is this truth that caused the prophet Daniel to exclaim: "But the people that do know their God shall be strong, and do exploits" (Daniel 11:32).

Jesus Christ put it this way: "And this is life eternal, that they might know thee the only true God, and Jesus Christ, whom thou has sent" (John 17:3). Eternal life is not merely the endless compounding of years. It is coming to know a Person in such a way that one experiences an entirely new kind of living. The Apostle Paul was still excited about new heights of experience in this kind of living after having received Christ in his life decades before. In his maturing years, from a prison cell, he writes: "But what things were gain to me, those things I counted loss for Christ. Yea doubtless, and I count all things but loss for the excellency of the knowledge of Christ Jesus my Lord. . . . That I may know him" (Philippians 3:7, 8, 10a). Knowing God is the secret of victorious life.

The Concepts of God
Some Modern Gods

No religion has ever been greater than its idea of God. More particularly, no life is greater than its understanding of God. This is why it is so basic to think right about God. It is my deep-seated conviction that the anemic American brand of Christianity today is at fault, at heart, in its low view of God. The appalling ignorance even among Christian people regarding the God in whom they profess belief, is nothing short of tragic. The French atheist, Voltaire, once said of his generation, "The Bible says, 'God made man in his own image,' and now man has returned the favor." A twentieth-century contemporary, J. B. Phillips, says the same to our generation in his incisive book *Your God Is Too Small*. Some of the modern gods he pictures are the Resident Policeman, the Parental Hangover, the Grand Old Man, the Meek and Mild, the Managing Director, the Perennial Grievance, the Pale Galilean, et cetera.

That mighty spokesman for God, A. W. Tozer, stated in his book *The Knowledge of the Holy*:

> It is my opinion that the Christian conception of God current in these middle years of the twentieth century is so decadent as to be utterly beneath the dignity of the most high God and actually to constitute for professed believers something amounting to a moral calamity.

On the positive side, he says,

> A right conception of God is basic not only to systematic theology, but to practical Christian living as well. It is to worship what the foundation is to the temple; where it is inadequate or out of plumb the whole structure must sooner or later collapse. I believe that there is scarcely an error in doctrine or a failure in applying Christian ethics that cannot be traced finally to imperfect and ignoble thoughts about God.

Surely, this is at the heart of the Word of the Lord in the Psalm when he said to the wicked man, "Thou thoughtest that I was altogether such an one as thyself" (Psalm 50:21).

I am driven to the question then: "What is God like?" And yet, as I begin my search in the things around me, I find at the outset that the question cannot be answered except to say that God is not like anything: that is, he is not exactly like anything or anybody. When we try to imagine what God is like, we must of necessity use that-which-is-not-God as the raw material for our minds to work on, and thus, whatever we visualize God to be, he is not, for we have constructed our image out of that which he has made, and what he has made is not God. If we insist upon trying to imagine him, we end up with an idol, made not with hands but with thoughts; and an idol of the mind is as offensive to God as an idol of the hands. You see, when we are left to ourselves, we tend immediately to reduce God to manageable terms. We want to get him where we can use him, or at least know where he is when we need him. We want a God we can in some measure control. It is at this precise point of thinking that Isaiah rises to the occasion to say:

> To whom then will ye liken God? or what likeness will ye compare unto him? The workman melteth and casteth an image, and the goldsmith spreadeth it over with gold, and casteth silver chains. He that is so impoverished that he hath no oblation chooseth a tree that will not rot; he seeketh a skillful workman to prepare a carved image, that shall not be moved. Have ye not known? Have ye not heard? Hath it not been told from the beginning? (Isaiah 40:18-21).

The Christ-likeness of God

There it is! "Hath it not been *told* you from the beginning?" That is the answer for which we are looking. How does man find out about God? Not by his imaginings. Not by a mere grotesque extension of something he already knows in creation. But by revelation. The seeker of old cried out: "Canst thou by searching find out God? canst thou find out the Almighty unto perfection? It is as high as heaven; what canst thou do? deeper than hell, what canst thou know?" (Job 11:7, 8). The answer of the Bible to Job's question of knowing God and what he is like is through Jesus Christ, our Lord. Listen to the Apostle John: "No man hath seen God at any time; the only begotten Son, who is in the bosom of the Father, he hath declared [exegeted, or expounded] him" (John 1:18). And Jesus himself said: "Neither knoweth any man the Father, save the Son, and he to whomsoever the Son will reveal him" (Matthew 11:27). Bearing right on this point, the Apostle Paul calls him "God . . . manifest in the flesh." Listen to these meaningful, majestic descriptions of Scripture:

> But in this the final age he has spoken to us in the Son whom he has made heir to the whole universe, and through whom he created all orders of existence: the Son who is the effulgence of God's splendor and the stamp of God's very being, and sustains the universe by his word of power (Hebrews 1:2, 3, NEB).

Listen again:

> Christ is the exact likeness of the unseen God. He existed before God made anything

at all, and, in fact, Christ himself is the Creator who made everything in heaven and earth, the things we can see and the things we can't; the spirit world with its kings and kingdoms, its rulers and authorities: all were made by Christ for his own use and glory. He was before all else began and it is his power that holds everything together (Colossians 1:15-17, TLB).

We see, then, that Jesus Christ both *is* the revelation of God and he *speaks* the revelation of God. He is the revelation of God in his matchless person, and he speaks the revelation of God in his mighty proclamations. If one would know what God is like, then let him look at Jesus Christ in his life and let him listen to him in his Word. We may learn of God from the entirety of the Bible, for Jesus Christ authenticated all of it as truth, but the epitome of the revelation is in the life and teachings of Christ himself.

Think not that I am come to destroy the law, or the prophets: I am not come to destroy, but to fulfill. For verily I say unto you, Till heaven and earth pass, one jot or one tittle shall in no wise pass from the law, till all be fulfilled (Matthew 5:17, 18).

The Characteristics of God
God Is Spirit

Obviously, we can only scratch the surface within the compass of such a short study, but perhaps it will be sufficient to whet our appetites to know more about this tremendous theme. One of the most basic things Jesus taught about the being of God is found in John 4:24: "God is spirit: and they that worship him must worship him in spirit and truth." In essence our Lord is saying that that which is real, that which is ultimate, is not material. God is not material. So God commanded Moses, "Thou shalt not make unto thee any carved image, or any likeness of anything that is in heaven above, or that is in the earth beneath, or that is in the water under the earth" (Exodus 20:4). As we noted earlier, Isaiah chides the image makers: "To whom then will ye liken God? Or what likeness will ye compare unto him?" (Isaiah 40:18). God is prior to and independent of all created things. All material things came into being by the Word of God; as Hebrews 11:3 states: "Things which are seen were not made of things which do appear." Therefore, God is not limited to a body. He is not tied to material things. God is spirit. Thus, those who would worship him, must worship him in spirit and in truth.

Now this should provide some tremendous insights for us today. We live in a day in which materialism seems to be the measure of all things. Things have a stranglehold on us. Men live for the present—for the things which they can see, touch, taste, and smell. We are the "now" generation who are willing to sacrifice eternal and spiritual values for temporal and material possessions. A "pot of porridge" is worth more to us than a "spiritual birthright." (Cf. Genesis 27.) For example, I find it much easier to exercise the minds of Christians about the need to get involved in a jogging program so they can lose weight and prolong their physical life, than to strip off the "spiritual weights" and to trim off the "sin pounds" so that they can enhance their spiritual welfare, both for now and for eternity. (Cf. Hebrews 12:2, 3.) Or again, when I listen to Christians talk about someone having their needs supplied by the Lord, invariably they are making reference to physical and material needs. How rarely today do people really become concerned about spiritual needs! In this affluent age, if Christians really believed that spiritual things are of ultimate importance, they would find themselves following the axiom of Matthew 6:19-21: "Lay not up for yourselves treasures upon earth, where moth and rust doth corrupt, and where thieves break through and steal: but lay up for yourselves treasure in heaven, where neither moth nor rust doth corrupt, and where thieves do not break through nor steal: for where your treasure is, there will your heart be also."

Check yourself on this for a moment. How often have you looked at someone who has a lovely home, two fine cars, a swimming pool, a camper, a cabin cruiser, et cetera, et cetera, and said: "My, how God has blessed you!" On the basis of what principles did you make that judgment? Since when is the blessing of God judged by material prosperity? On that basis, the Mafia are among the most blessed of God. How different is this kind of judgment from that of the early apostles and post-apostolic fathers who gladly sacrificed all that they had, including their very lives which they allowed to be burned at the stake, while they sang praises to their great God and King. How different is the contemporary judgment of God's blessing from that of the Son of Man himself, who said: "If any man will come after me, let him deny himself, and take up his cross daily, and follow me. For whosoever would save his life shall lose it; but whosoever will lose his life for my sake, the same shall save it" (Luke 9:23, 24). There is a chorus that used to be sung by young people:

> With eternity's values in view, Lord,
> With eternity's values in view:
> May I do each day's work for Jesus,
> With eternity's values in view.

If any of us has a lingering ray of hope for this earth, and material things, let him contemplate the stark reality that nuclear fission has demonstrated the destructibility of matter. As Dr. Merrill Tenney has graphically stated: "One nervous finger on the wrong switch could precipitate an atomic war which would not simply lay the world in ruins, as the barbarians sacked and burned Rome and its sister cities, but would dissolve it in fire and death, leaving only a desert so radioactive that no living thing could survive. The scientific inventiveness which has provided men with control over the powers of nature, has accelerated his economic, intellectual, and social development, but in what direction will it take him? Is he only moving faster toward destruction?"

And it is just such a destruction which the Scriptures predict for this material planet:

> But the day of the Lord will come as a thief in the night; in which the heavens shall pass away with a great noise, and the elements

shall melt with fervent heat, the earth also and the works that are therein shall be burned up. Seeing then that all these things shall be dissolved, what manner of persons ought ye to be in all holy conversation and godliness, looking for and hasting unto the coming of the day of God, wherein the heavens being on fire shall be dissolved, and the elements shall melt with fervent heat? (2 Peter 3:10-12).

This certainly should have something to say to us who find ourselves inextricably engaged in the stockpiling of material things.

Yet, I would hasten to say that this threatening of the imminent destruction of our present world system is a welcome discovery because it has brought to mind far more clearly than ever before, spiritual values—incapable of physical destruction. In former days, it has been popular to talk of spiritual values as shadowy and unsubstantial, and the physical as solid and real and reliable. But with the evidence of the imminent universal destructibility of matter, the tables are turned. The physical world which has seemed so real and tangible is getting most uncomfortably unreliable. Man is inclined to say that maybe reality lies in another realm altogether. It is becoming more and more clear that reality is outside the realm of things that can be seen or measured in a test tube, and this is exactly the testimony of Scripture: "Now faith is the substance of things hoped for, the evidence of things not seen . . . Through faith we understand that the worlds were framed by the Word of God, so that things which are seen were not made of things which do appear" (Hebrews 11:1, 3). One who truly understands what God is like will find himself giving more and more attention to the spiritual and less and less importance to the material. The essence of reality is spiritual, not material. "God is a spirit: and they that worship him must worship him in spirit and in truth" (John 4:24).

We have thought about God's relation to created things—the material universe—and learned that he is before them all and independent of them all. In like manner, God is before and beyond time. Time and space were both created by God. Just as God was continuously existing before there was any material creation, so he continuously existed before there was time. The original text of John 1:1 clearly displays in the verb tenses that when the beginning of time was, at that time God was already continuously existing. Moses said: "Before the mountains were brought forth, or ever thou hadst formed the earth and the world, even from everlasting to everlasting, thou art God" (Psalm 90:2). Time marks the beginning of created existence, and because God never began to exist, it can have no application to him. In fact, the word "began" is a quite human word and can have no meaning for the high and lofty One that inhabiteth eternity.

God Is Timeless

Not only is God before time, and thus there is no beginning with him; likewise, there is no succession of events with him. We know past, present, and future, but God is spoken of as existing in the "eternal present." There is no past and no future with him. Just as he is not limited by a physical body in space, so he is not limited by succession of moments, called time. When time words occur in the Scriptures, they refer to our time, not to his. We know things as "before" and "after" but not so with God. He has already lived all our tomorrows as he has lived all our yesterdays. C. S. Lewis suggests that we think of a sheet of paper infinitely extended. That would be eternity. Then, on the paper, draw a short line to represent time. As the line begins and ends on that infinite expanse, so time began in God and will end in him. This is why God can say, "I am God, and there is none like me, declaring the end from the beginning" (Isaiah 46:9b, 10a).

The practical implications of this truth about God are marvelous to contemplate.

God knows my tomorrows as well as he knows my today. The God who is leading me through today will not be caught by surprise tomorrow. The events of today in my life are his preparation for my tomorrows. Again, think of the eternity of God from another standpoint. Many people have had trouble with the idea of God attending to the prayers of several hundred million beings who are all addressing him at the same moment. The problem, of course, is with those words "at the same moment." But God is not bound by time. His life does not consist of moments following one upon another. C. S. Lewis comments that any time of day or night from the beginning of the world is always *present* for him. God has all eternity to listen to the split second of prayer put up by a pilot as his plane crashes in flames.

There is coming a day when those who have been born of God through Jesus Christ will experience in its fullness the eternity for which we have been born. We have been made for eternity, and right now we are living on the edge of it. So little time and so much to do is a frustrating situation. But this will not always be the case. God has made us for something far better. Yes, "When we've been there ten thousand years, bright shining as the sun, we've no less days to sing God's praise than when we first begun."

Now, let's think briefly of another attribute of God; namely, his infinitude. This is one of the most difficult concepts to understand, for the very contemplation of it reveals how feeble the human mind is to grasp such greatness. All our thoughts about him will be less than he, and our loftiest utterances will be trivialities in comparison with him. But let us stretch our minds to understand, knowing that "the secret things belong unto the Lord our God: but those things which are revealed belong unto us and to our children forever" (Deuteronomy 29:29). God has told us these things that we might know him better.

God Is Limitless

Now, infinitude, of course, means limitlessness, and when we say that God is infinite, we mean that he knows no bounds. Whatever God is and all that God is, he is without limit. Now, let's apply this to a couple of areas.

God is infinite in knowledge. By this we mean that everything, actual and possible, from all eternity is known by him, and everyone is known completely as to his needs, actual condition, past and future possibilities. As the writer to the Hebrews states, "And before him no creature is hidden, but all are open and laid bare to the eyes of him with whom we have to do" (Hebrews 4:3, RSV). The implications of this truth lie in two areas. In relation to God, this means that he has not, need not, indeed cannot learn anything new. He has never discovered anything and has never been amazed or taken by surprise. Since he is also changeless, this perfect knowledge will not fail, and since he is infinite, it has no limitations. Nothing ever grows dim in his knowledge, and he never knows anything better than any other thing. As this truth relates to men, it means that he knows you better than you know yourself, and if you would know yourself, it must be by knowing him.

This fact is illustrated in the experience recorded in John 21:15-17, as the risen Lord seeks to restore the denying Peter to fellowship with himself.

> So when they had dined, Jesus saith to Simon Peter, Simon son of Jonas, lovest thou me more than these? He saith unto him, Yea, Lord; thou knowest that I love thee. He saith unto him, Feed my lambs. He saith to him again the second time, Simon, son of Jonas, lovest thou me? He saith unto him, Yea, Lord, thou knowest that I love thee. He saith unto him, Feed my sheep. He saith unto him

the third time, Simon, son of Jonas, lovest thou me? Peter was grieved because he said unto him the third time, Lovest thou me? And he said unto him, Lord, thou knowest all things; thou knowest that I love thee. Jesus saith unto him, Feed my sheep.

As he raises the threefold question, "Simon, do you love me more than these?" and receives the response, he is not actually seeking information, but trying to lead Peter to an awareness first of his need, and then of his relationship with Jesus Christ. The Lord knew even before Peter responded that Peter loved him, but the problem was Peter himself; he was not sure whether he loved the Lord, in the light of recent circumstances. This was the Lord's way of confirming this to Peter. As Peter came to know Jesus Christ better, he came to know himself better.

Further implications of this truth as it relates to men are as follows: Because he perfectly knows us, nothing out of the past can cause him to change his mind about us, for he knew our past when he saved us. "While we were yet helpless, at the right time Christ died for the ungodly . . . God shows his love for us in that while we were yet sinners Christ died for us" (Romans 5:6, 8, RSV).

Again, because he perfectly knows us, nothing in the present can threaten us, for he knew our needs fully when he saved us and made full provision for them. "Who shall bring any charge against God's elect? It is God who justifies; who is to condemn?" (Romans 8:33, RSV).

And then again, because he perfectly knows us,

nothing in the future can undo his work, for not only does he know the future, he is eternal and therefore he controls the future. It holds no mystery for him. Thus Paul writes, "For I am sure that neither death, nor life, nor angels, nor principalities, nor things present, nor things to come, nor powers, nor height, nor depth, nor anything else in all creation, will be able to separate us from the love of God in Christ Jesus our Lord" (Romans 8:38, 39, RSV).

God is infinite in power. We refer to this as his omnipotence, meaning that he has unlimited resources of power and is unlimited in his exercise of it, that is, in his ability to carry out his purposes. All of the human resources of power for both constructive and destructive purposes, whether actually controlled by or potentially known by men, even when combined, do not represent as much power as the omnipotence of God. In the Scriptures, this truth is repeatedly emphasized by the use of the term "almighty," which means, "He who possesses or holds on to everything." "I am the Lord and there is no other, besides me there is no God; I gird you, though you do not know me, that men may know, from the rising of the sun and from the west, that there is none besides me; I am the Lord, and there is no other. I form light and create darkness, I make weal and create woe. I am the Lord, who do all these things" (Isaiah 45:5-7, RSV). And again, he says, "Behold, I am the Lord, the God of all flesh: is anything too hard for me?" (Jeremiah 32:27). The implications of the omnipotence of God for our practical everyday life are many. Let us consider a few.

That God is omnipotent means that there is no power or will that can ultimately thwart his purposes. Perhaps the most dramatic illustration of this is found by comparing the words of the Psalmist and the words of Peter as recorded in his Pentecostal sermon. The Psalmist says, "Surely the wrath of man shall praise thee; the residue of wrath thou wilt gird upon thee" (Psalm 76:10). Both prove to be true in the death of Christ as Peter says on Pentecost:

> Men of Israel, hear these words: Jesus of Nazareth, a man attested to you by God with mighty works and wonders and signs which God did through him in your midst, as you yourselves know—this Jesus, delivered up according to the definite plan and foreknowledge of God, you crucified and killed by the hands of lawless men. But God raised him up, having loosed the pangs of death, because it was not possible for him to be held by it (Acts 2:22-24, RSV).

Even that which appeared to be a triumph of Satan and satanically inspired men, God turned to the accomplishment of his own will.

Again, this truth means that there is no work that God undertakes that he cannot fulfill. "I am sure that he who began a good work in you will bring it to completion at the day of Jesus Christ," says Paul in Philippians 1:6 (RSV). Again, "I know whom I have believed and I am sure that he is able to guard until that Day what has been entrusted to me. Wherefore, he is able also to save them to the uttermost that come unto God by him, seeing he ever liveth to make intercession for them" (2 Timothy 1:12, RSV, and Hebrews 7:25). This also means that no matter how great the work he performs, his resources are not depleted. No matter how much energy he expends, he is not exhausted or in need of renewed strength. Thus, though he is always giving, he never gives away, for all he gives remains his own and returns to him again.

Let us complete our discourse in the majestic fortieth chapter of Isaiah where we started. It tells the story of a whipped and discouraged people, Israel, from whom the Babylonian captivity had taken its toll. Difficulties loomed overwhelmingly. Depression set in. There were enemies within and without. At this time, doubts began to rise about God's concern. When distress or suffering becomes prolonged, it is easy to think that God has forgotten or is indifferent. Consequently, the people cry out in verse 27 that their way is hidden from the Lord. He doesn't see what has happened to them, and their cause has not been righteously judged by God. Their right has been disregarded by their God, they believe.

God Is Understanding

Now how does God meet this rebellious and insolent spirit? By giving them a thorough tongue-lashing? No, the prophet does not exhort the people to rouse themselves from their defeatism. That is like whipping a jaded horse. Rather, he tells them about their God. Verse 28 tells them all about what God is like. He is the everlasting God, above time, but in all the events of history.

He is sovereign, the Lord of time and the Lord of space. He is one who doesn't grow faint as men do who neglect to take repeated nourishment. He doesn't become weary like a man who has exhausted his capacity for work by overexertion. In fact, Jehovah is so far from becoming faint that it is he who gives strength to the fainting. He has unfathomable understanding. He is in possession of the infallible criteria for determining the right point of time at which to interpose his aid. Thus, the writer says that they who will wait upon the Lord, those who will take a good long look at him, shall renew their strength, and the Hebrew word here means to "exchange"; that is, they shall exchange their weakness for his strength. It is to the waiting mentality that increases of strength are promised. People that take time to contemplate what God is like shall exchange their weakness for his strength. They shall mount up with wings like eagles. The little child who tries to fly, quickly learns the lesson that no amount of arm-flailing ever lifted a person even a fraction of an inch off the ground. In fact, the wonder of bird flight remained a mystery during the first centuries, and we still do not completely understand how birds fly—for instance, the marvelous ease of an eagle's gravity-defying flight, the sheer grandeur and grace of his mounting through the air. We know that eagles soar to great altitudes. In fact, one once was observed flying at 25,000 feet, off Mt. Everest. The eagle appears to be free from the pull of gravity, but not so. The gravity is exerting a constant downward pull upon him, but there is a greater force that opposes it, with the result that gravity is counteracted and the bird is pushed upwards.

So it is with us; as we focus our attention on what God is like, we shall not be free from the pull of gravity that would have us become enmeshed in the tyranny of things in this world, but we shall find that there is a greater force that opposes it, with the result that this gravity is counteracted and we soar with God in the heavenlies. "We all, with unveiled face, beholding as in a mirror the glory of the Lord, are changed into the same image from glory to glory, even as by the spirit of the Lord" (2 Corinthians 3:18).

THE HOLINESS OF GOD

William F. Kerr
Th.D.

Is history repeating itself in theology today? It would appear so. From all indications on the theological and ecclesiastical scene it would seem that we have not profited from the lessons which history has tried to teach us. We appear to have blindly passed by the very lessons which our theological and ecclesiastical fathers sought to teach us and which caused them much pain and sacrifice to learn. For it appears that we are again entering that vicious circle of theological history which will lead ultimately to liberalism or, if not to liberalism within our own ranks, at least to a debilitated and emaciated conservatism. And this, in turn, will lead to an attitude of compromise and indifference toward liberalism.

But just what are the lessons which theological and ecclesiastical history wants to teach us? These lessons can be reduced fundamentally to one basic concept, namely, the overoccupation with divine love as foundational to all of God's dealings with sinful man. As A. H. Strong, at the turn of the century, so well stated in the preface to his *Systematic Theology* (p. x):

> I desire especially to call attention to the section on Perfection, and the Attributes therein involved, because I believe that the recent merging of Holiness in Love, and the practical denial that Righteousness is fundamental in God's nature, are responsible for the utilitarian views of law and the superficial views of sin which now prevail in some systems of theology. There can be no proper doctrine of the atonement and no proper doctrine of retribution, so long as Holiness is refused its pre-eminence. Love must have a norm or standard, and this norm or standard can be found only in Holiness."

And then, speaking of theological conditions of his day, he continues,

> The theology of our day needs a new view of the Righteous One.

But what about the theology of our own day? Are we being swamped today with an overemphasis upon and a distortion of divine love?

Has the literature on love as the essential attribute of God's nature and as the necessary attitude and motivation for Christian action so flooded our Christian magazines and bookstands that we can hardly contemplate any other subject?

In both liberal and evangelical circles we are being reminded that, as fundamentalists, we are unlovely and unloving. It is for this reason that we are being forced today to demand a biblical definition of love as an attribute of God and a clearer explanation of its relationship to God's other attributes and actions. And we are being driven to ask in the language of Dr. Strong: "Does not Divine Love demand a norm or standard? And is not the norm or standard to be found only in the doctrine of the Divine Holiness as the ground of God's actions?" And we hasten to answer our own inquiry in the affirmative.

Such an answer will remind us that the past has taught us or should have taught us that an overemphasis upon or a distortion of divine love has obscured God's holiness. It has thus consequently reduced sin to a misdemeanor, love to sheer sentimentality, conduct to moral indifference, and the supernatural to the ordinary workings of the mechanics of nature. Carl F. H. Henry calls to our attention the fact that in such an overoccupation with or distortion of divine love the "divine holiness is subordinated to the divine love whenever it is thought that God pampers with sin, or that He reacts so mildly that man is able to redeem himself in God's sight." (*Notes on the Doctrine of God*, p. 107). And then he adds: "Such a spirit was abroad in the religious modernism which arose in the century past within the doors of Protestant churches." He concludes with this trenchant statement: "Such liberalism banished from modern theology the notions of substitutionary atonement, supernatural regeneration, human depravity, special revelation and, along with this, the holiness of God conceived in any adequate manner" (p. 108).

In the light of such a history of the misunderstanding of God's basic attribute of holiness and the misapplication of his attribute of love, should we not ask ourselves another vital question, and that question is: "Are we not in imminent danger of initiating the same vicious theological circle by our overemphasis on divine love, which led in the past to liberalism in our churches, and should we not call modern evangelicalism, or at least conservatives, back to the faith of their fathers, who emphasized that divine love must be grounded in divine holiness?" For it was an evangelical theologian, E. G. Robinson, the theology teacher of A. H. Strong, who called American theology back to a consideration of God's holiness when liberalism was sweeping the churches with its overemphasis upon divine love. Robinson recognized the dangers inherent in overoccupation with God's love as the ground of all his actions and the expression of his nature. He realized that the only healthy attitude and the only way to express clearly the biblical teaching was to make God's holiness the ground of his actions toward men both in love and in justice.

For this reason it is well for us to examine what the biblical evidence and teaching is concerning this fundamental attribute of God's nature.

We shall consider the biblical teaching on the

importance of the divine holiness under three categories.

Its Delineation

The emphasis placed by the Bible on the holiness of God leads us to express, in the words of A. H. Strong, that "holiness is the fundamental and essential attribute of the nature of God." Indeed, it is the all-embracing attribute of God and forms the ground in which all his other attributes inhere and thus becomes the basis for the expression of all of his other attributes and actions.

The importance which the Bible places upon this attribute can be delineated in the following three ways:

The Perfection of His Attributes

As one reads the Word of God he is struck by the repeated emphasis upon the holiness of God. For instance, in that magnificent portion of Isaiah's prophecy in which the prophet saw the Lord, high and lifted up, we read:

In the year that King Uzziah died I saw also the Lord sitting upon a throne, high and lifted up, and his train filled the temple. Above it stood the seraphim: each one had six wings; with twain he covered his face, and with twain he covered his feet, and with twain he did fly. And one cried unto another, and said, Holy, holy, holy, is the Lord of hosts: the whole earth is full of his glory. And the posts of the door moved at the voice of him that cried, and the house was filled with smoke (Isaiah 6:1-4).

And, again, in the closing prophetic book of the Bible we read: "And the four beasts had each of them six wings about him; and they were full of eyes within: and they rest not day and night, saying, Holy, holy, holy, Lord God Almighty, which was, and is, and is to come" (Revelation 4:8).

So comprehensive is the attribute of holiness in reference to God's nature that we will find it only emphasized in the repetition of his title as in the verses quoted above. For in no place in the Word of God do we read such repetitions as "Love, love, love" or "Truth, truth, truth" in reference to God's nature. No, God's holiness is so foundational to his nature that the very title used to describe him is, "Holy, holy, holy."

However, not only do we see his holiness emphasized in the titles applied to him but we also see it in the name by which he is known. In Psalm 111:9 we note: "He sent redemption unto his people: he hath commanded his covenant forever: Holy and reverend is his name." The awesomeness of God's name is found in his holiness. Isaiah testifies to this when he writes: "For thus saith the high and lofty One that inhabiteth eternity, whose name is Holy; . . ." (Isaiah 57:15).

The very name of God demands that his dwelling place be holy. Verse after verse of Scripture floods one's mind to verify this. Psalm 20:6 states: "Now know I that the Lord saveth his anointed; he will hear him from his holy heaven with the saving strength of his right hand." Or as the psalmist says again: "Exalt the Lord our God, and worship at his holy hill: for the Lord our God is holy" (Psalm 99:9). Isaiah, the great prophet of God's holiness, also supports the contention that God's residence is holy, when he states: ". . . I dwell in the high and holy place, with him also that is of a contrite and humble spirit . . " (Isaiah 57:15).

In the light of such evidence it is difficult for us to see how any other attribute of God can be as comprehensive in its definition of God's nature as that of his holiness. No other attribute appears to stand on the same level with God's holiness nor is any other one emphasized to the same degree. For it is indeed the all-embracing attribute of God. Louis Berkhof, the renowned Reformed theologian, witnesses to the fundamental importance of the attribute of God's holiness when he writes: "God's holiness is rather something that is co-extensive with and applicable to everything that can be predicated of God" (*Systematic Theology*, p. 73). And thus, as far as we are concerned, it portrays God's majestic nature, and creates in each one of his creatures that sense of genuine awe and awfulness that teaches each one that he is in the presence of a holy God. And such a sense of God's holiness impresses us with the fact of our own corruption and evil. This is especially seen as we note another manifestation of God's holiness.

The Purity of His Being

Both the perfection of God's attributes and the purity of his being emphasize the essential fact of

God's holiness. For the basic idea of purity is that of separation from evil. God abhors sin. In his presence no darkness nor evil can dwell. He cannot countenance iniquity. Habakkuk describes the purity of God's being in these words: "Thou art of purer eyes than to behold evil, and canst not look on iniquity; wherefore lookest thou upon them that deal treacherously, and holdest thy tongue when the wicked devoureth the man that is more righteous than he?" (Habakkuk 1:13). This is also corroborated by the book of Job when it states: "Therefore hearken unto me, ye men of understanding; far be it from God, that he should do wickedness; and from the Almighty, that he should commit iniquity" (Job 34:10).

Such a concept of the Divine abhorrence of sin carries with it an ethical truth that in God's relationships with man, he convicts man of his utter sinfulness. This was certainly Isaiah's reaction when he said: "Then said I, Woe is me! for I am undone; because I am a man of unclean lips, and I dwell in the midst of a people of unclean lips; for mine eyes have seen the King, the Lord of hosts" (Isaiah 6:5). And, like Isaiah of old, each one of us needs to recognize that he is utterly sinful and undone and in deep heart need of cleansing such as Isaiah experienced: "Then flew one of the seraphim unto me, having a live coal in his hand, which he had taken with the tongs from off the altar: And he laid it upon my mouth, and said, Lo, this hath touched thy lips; and thine iniquity is taken away, and thy sin purged" (Isaiah 6:6, 7). Such cleansing is, of course, available to each one in the sacrifice of that Holy One of God, even the Lord Jesus. The writer to the Hebrews writes: ". . . when he had by himself purged our sins, sat down on the right hand of the Majesty on high" (Hebrews 1:3). And, in another place, he writes: "Wherefore he is able also to save them to the uttermost that come unto God by him, seeing he ever liveth to make intercession for them" (Hebrews 7:25).

However, not only is there a provision for the unbeliever's conviction of sin and his cleansing from sin but there is also a provision for the believer's cleansing from the sins that enter his life. In the first letter of John we read: "If we confess our sins, he is faithful and just to forgive us our sins, and to cleanse us from all unrighteousness" (1 John 1:9). And such cleansing is a necessary follow-through of our realization of the awful holiness of God, which challenges man to a life of victorious, holy living. A holy God put it in these words to Moses, when he said: "For I am the Lord your God: ye shall therefore sanctify yourselves, and ye shall be holy, for I am holy . . . For I am the Lord that bringeth you up out of the land of Egypt, to be your God: ye shall therefore be holy, for I am holy" (Leviticus 11:44, 45). A holy God demands a holy people. He makes provision for our holiness through our salvation by faith in Christ and he gives power for our daily progress in sanctification by the empowerment and enablement of the Holy Spirit. There is no substitute for holy living because we belong to a holy God. And yet, there are too many people, members of evangelical churches today, who prefer to overlook the demands of a holy God upon their lives.

Professing belief in the Word of God and salvation in Christ, they neglect the application of God's holiness to everyday life and living. They desire to close the door to God's holiness in certain areas of their lives. They take lightly the admonition of Peter: "But as he which hath called you is holy, so be ye holy in all manner of conversation; because it is written, Be ye holy, for I am holy" (1 Peter 1:15, 16). Revival, therefore, is the need of the hour; a revival of the concept of the awe and majesty of God's holiness. And with this revival must come a corresponding application of the truth of God's holiness to the lives of the believers.

Such a truth leads us to a consideration of the third way in which the Bible emphasizes the importance of the attribute of God's holiness.

The Purposiveness of His Actions

Every action of God is grounded in his holiness. It is basic both to his goodness and grace as well as his justice and wrath. It is so fundamental in these areas that to confuse it with his love as the basis for his actions is to bring God's nature under question and to reduce his saving, redeeming acts to the mere whims of sentimentality.

For it is only as God reacts through his holiness toward unbelieving men that he must react in love to save them. It is his holiness that makes the meaning of his love for men comprehensible. Unless we see him move in love because of his holiness, the words of John make no sense when he says: "For God so loved the world, that he gave his only begotten Son, that whosoever believeth in him should not perish, but have everlasting life" (John 3:16).

Conversely, it is only as God reacts through his holiness toward unbelieving men that he must react in justice to punish them. If God is not holy, why then should he punish those who reject his love, spurn his grace, and revel in their sinful pleasures? And what meaning can the words of Paul have when he states: "For the wages of sin is death. . . ." (Romans 6:23)? Or, again, when he concluded: "Now we know that what things soever the law saith, it saith to them who are under the law; that every mouth may be stopped, and all the world may become guilty before God" (Romans 3:19)?

There could be no rationale to the purposiveness of God's action either in redeeming men in love or condemning men in justice unless this purposiveness was grounded or based in his holiness.

Its Demonstration

The second category under which we desire to study the holiness of God is that of its demonstration in his actions. This is directly based upon what we have said about the purposiveness of his actions. However, we must develop the thought further and show that the demonstration of God's holiness must be found in himself and his nature. It implies the revelation of his moral law to his creatures and the reconciling of these creatures to fellowship with himself through the redemptive work of Christ at Calvary. Such a demonstration of God's holiness can be seen in three aspects.

The Law of God

The moral law of God is pictured in the Scriptures as an exhibition of God's holiness. For in God's law we see the holiness of God in tangible, visible form. Only a holy God, who is absolutely holy, could reveal his demands legally and hold man accountable for their observation and obedience. A. H. Strong notes: "But we need especially to emphasize the fact that this law . . . is an expression of the moral nature of God, and therefore of God's holiness, the fundamental attribute of that nature; . ." (*Systematic Theology*, p. 537). Paul bears out this view of the law when, in writing to the Romans, he notes: "Wherefore the law is holy, and the commandment holy, and just, and good" (Romans 7:12). And the psalmist bears the same testimony:

> The law of the Lord is perfect, converting the soul: the testimony of the Lord is sure, making wise the simple. The statutes of the Lord are right, rejoicing the heart: the commandment of the Lord is pure, enlightening the eyes. The fear of the Lord is clean, enduring forever: the judgments of the Lord are true and righteous altogether (Psalm 19:7-9).

God's moral law is best known to us, in part, in the Ten Commandments. But God's moral law goes even deeper than the Ten Commandments as is seen in the reinterpretation of that law in the words of Christ in the Sermon on the Mount. And by that very reinterpretation we are made aware that in the age of grace, God has not abrogated his law. Rather, he has more fully explained it and made it richer by the demands which it makes upon believers for the living of a holy life.

There are many believers today who would like to relegate the Sermon on the Mount to the future kingdom. They tell us it will be God's standard in that day and we believe that. However, we cannot so easily sidestep the demands of God's moral law, as seen in the Sermon on the Mount. We need to recognize that Christ's words in the Sermon demand a heart attitude that will demonstrate spirituality in keeping with the demands of that law. For in comparing the law of Moses with the words of Christ we note the more profound intent and meaning which Christ gave to God's moral law. Take, for instance, these words:

> Ye have heard that it was said by them of old time, Thou shalt not kill; and whosoever shall kill shall be in danger of the judgment: but I say unto you, That whosoever is angry with his brother without a cause shall be in danger of the judgment; and whosoever shall say to his brother, Raca, shall be in danger of the council (Matthew 5:21, 22).

Such a profound concept of God's moral law forming, as it does, a holy self-revelation of God, cannot be treated lightly by us. Therefore, just as Christ is, so we ought to be and want to be. For, as Paul says, "Christ is the end of the law for righteousness to every one that believeth" (Romans 10:4). By the redemptive grace of God, through faith in Christ, and the divine enablement of the Holy Spirit, we want to live a holy life before a holy God.

The Love of God

The holiness of God is also demonstrated in his love. And it is here that we come into sharpest conflict with some modern-day views of God's actions in reconciling man to himself. For there are many among modern evangelicals who ground the atoning work of Christ in the love of God rather than in the holiness of God. To do so is to miss the real impact of the Bible's teaching concerning both the holiness of God and the redemptive work of Christ. To quote Strong again: "There can be no proper doctrine of the atonement and no proper doctrine of retribution, so long as Holiness is refused its preeminence. Love must have a norm or standard, and this norm or standard can be found only in Holiness" (*Systematic Theology*, p. x).

The importance of this concept of God's holiness as the ground of God's redemptive love in Christ is realized when we notice that the Bible teaches that the justice of God demands the punishment of the sinner. How then, we ask, can God justify the sinner? Is there an insoluble tension in God? Are his love and holiness in grave tension so that there is conflict within God's nature?

Such appears to be the position of Nels F. S. Ferre. I recall hearing him lecture a number of years ago and he stated, at that time, that there was a tension within God's nature. His holiness condemned sinning man; his love wanted to forgive men. How could this tension be finally resolved? Only as God's love ultimately triumphed and all sinning creatures were restored to God. This, of course, is simply universalism which teaches that all sinning, evil creatures—men and angels—will ultimately be saved.

But is this how the Word of God resolves the so-called tension and justifies the sinner? Not at all! The Word of God knows of no tension in God's nature. Rather, it clearly states that the holiness of God—God's essential attribute—is the ground or basis of both his justice and his love. The justice of God must punish sin; the love of God wants to forgive sin. And the Word of God clearly reveals that both of these are properly kept in balance as God's holiness forms the basis of God's action in both.

Therefore, our original question, "How can God justify the sinner?" finds its answer in the Scriptures. Paul writes:

> For all have sinned and come short of the glory of God; being justified freely by his grace through the redemption that is in Christ Jesus: whom God hath set forth to be a propitiation through faith in his blood, to declare his righteousness for the remission of sins that are past, through the forbearance of God; to declare, I say, at this time his righteousness: that he might be just, and the justifier of him which believeth in Jesus (Romans 3:23-26).

In order to preserve his justice, a holy God has sent his own Son into the world to die for sinning men. He bore the full brunt of the wrath and justice of God against the sins of the world in his own body on the tree. He became man's substitute and he satisfied the holy justice of God. When, therefore, man accepts Christ as Savior, he finds forgiveness of sin and is reconciled to God. The demands of God's law and holiness are satisfied and the love of God moves in redeeming and forgiving grace. In this way, and in this way alone, can God "be just and the justifier of him which believeth in Jesus." There is thus no tension in God; there is rather the satisfaction of God's justice through Christ's death and the manifestation of God's love as he forgives the repentant, believing sinner. And if man refuses to believe, then God has satisfied his justice by condemning him to an eternal hell.

However, if love is made the basis for the atonement, then the atonement must be termed as irrational and capricious. For, as Strong so ably states: "Holiness cannot be love, because love is irrational and capricious except as it has a standard by which it is regulated, and this standard cannot be itself love, but must be holiness" (*Systematic Theology*, p. 271). And the reason why love is irrational and capricious is seen by the thinking of Ferre, above. To him, the justice of God can ultimately be ignored because the love of God overcomes it in forgiving all sinning creatures and restoring them to God's favor. But a love which is regulated by the standard of holiness will carefully guard God's justice by demanding the punishment of the unrepentant sinner and the forgiveness of the repentant, believing sinner.

This view of God's love will preserve it against degenerating into a mere sentimentalism which allows the sinner to defy God, despise his grace, and still gain ultimate reconciliation with God in eternity. And it is just such a concept of love as mere sentimentalism which is in danger of being advocated by many evangelicals today. And because of this we need to be reminded of the importance of God's holiness as the ground of the atonement and as the standard which regulates God's loving actions. For, as Strong also notes, the holiness of God is the track upon which the train of his love runs.

The advocacy of love, apart from the standard of God's holiness, will cause the lowering of the bars of conduct among believers. And many modern evangelicals are advancing just such a view. This writer believes that such a view finds its basis in a concept of love which is irrational and capricious. It reduces love to sentimentality and is in danger of reducing conduct to convenience.

Let us be very careful, therefore, to base our concept of God's love and his loving actions in the attribute of his holiness. And in that way our conduct will be carefully guarded.

The Life Through God

Not only do you find the holiness of God demonstrated in his law and in his love but you find it also in the life through God. For here, in a sense, is the combination of both to be found in the believer. The law of God reveals his holy nature; the love of God makes available that holy nature through his forgiving grace in Christ. When this forgiveness is appropriated, there is new life for the sinner from God.

This is seen when we notice that by faith in Christ we are made new creations in him. Paul writes: "Therefore, if any man be in Christ, he is a new creature; old things are passed away; behold, all things are become new" (2 Corinthians 5:17). And, again: "And have put on the new man, which is renewed in knowledge after the image of him that created him" (Colossians 3:10). Also: "And that ye put on the new man, which after God is created in righteousness and true holiness" (Ephesians 4:24).

In light of the demands of God's holiness and the new life which can be had by faith in Christ, some personal questions need to be asked. Are you a new creation in Christ Jesus? Have you personally accepted him as your Savior? If you have, are you living as you ought to live? Or have you let down the bars of holy conduct? Have your old lusts, desires, ambitions been brought into subservience to Christ? Or have you become indifferent to the demands of a holy God, who desires from you a holy life?

Its Duty

We have tried to show previously in many ways that the doctrine of the holiness of God has a practical application to the lives of the believers. It must have an effect upon our lives. If it does not, then it becomes a mere matter of academic interest and theological curiosity. For that reason we believe that it is most practical in its relationships.

To fail to apply God's holiness to the lives of believers is to run the risk of falling prey to all kinds of doctrinal deviations or conflicts in conduct. Thus it is mandatory for the believer to heed scriptural injunctions such as those found in Leviticus 11:45b: ". . . ye shall therefore be holy, for I am holy." Or, as found in 1 Peter 1:15, 16: "But as he which hath called you is holy, so be ye holy in all manner of conversation; because it is written, Be ye holy; for I am holy."

The believer, to be holy, will live a life characterized by four principles.

He Will Be a Crucified Man

When our Lord Jesus was nailed to the cross in God's judgment on sin, those who believe in him were also nailed there. This is called the principle of identification and is a most important biblical principle for believers. It is a principle which the believer must recognize if he is to live as holy unto God. Paul mentions the principle on several occasions. Writing to the Romans, he says: "Knowing this, that our old man is crucified with him, that the body of sin might be destroyed, that henceforth we should not serve sin" (Romans 6:6). And in Galatians 2:20: "I am crucified with Christ; nevertheless I live, yet not I, but Christ liveth in me; and the life which I now live in the flesh I live by the faith of the Son of God."

In these two principles, the Spirit of God tells us

that we have been crucified with Christ. We were nailed to the cross with him. The body of sin in us, by faith in Christ, has been rendered inoperative. Our lives should be lives of victory. Hence the questions come to us: "Do we really know that this has been accomplished for us? Do we reckon these things to be true?" Have we yielded our "members as instruments of righteousness unto God?"

Such a principle of identification means that we should crucify all fleshly affections and lusts. Paul writes: "And they that are Christ's have crucified the flesh with the affections and lusts. If we live in the Spirit, let us also walk in the Spirit. Let us not be desirous of vainglory, provoking one another, envying one another" (Galatians 5:24-26).

All our pride, desire for prestige, political chicanery and fleshly idols must be brought into submission to Christ. The leadership of God's Spirit in the living of a godly, humble life will be evident. Our desires and ambitions will be God-directed.

This principle also demands that our ethical standard in every area of life be above reproach. For our Lord laid down a principle: "Therefore all things whatsoever ye would that men should do to you, do ye even so to them: for this is the law and the prophets" (Matthew 7:12). Certainly, the believer cannot be guilty of doing any less than this. He does not do it out of personal strength but by the enabling of the Holy Spirit. But he does it that he may glorify his Lord and Master.

Ethical standards above reproach must characterize every believer. But they must especially characterize those of us who hold very dear and very precious the whole counsel of God's Word.

We who are separatists—so-called—must above all be most meticulous in the observance of the highest Christian ethical standards. We must be very careful that nothing that we do and nothing that we say shall ever be questioned on an ethical, Christian basis. Sometimes we are so keen in pursuing our separatist position that we use methods, procedures, and statements that can be gravely questioned as unethical. We must always withhold judgment until all the facts are in. Only in such a way can our ethical standards measure up to the regulations of the Bible. Only in such a way can we demonstrate that our holiness in life measures up to the demands of a holy God. Only in such a way can we show that we have been crucified with Christ and that being identified with him our lives are Christlike.

He Will Be a Committed Man

A crucified man—identified with Christ in his crucifixion—will be wholly committed and yielded to Christ. He will know experientially and exhibit practically in his life the meaning of Romans 12:1, 2: "I beseech you therefore, brethren, by the mercies of God, that ye present your bodies a living sacrifice, holy, acceptable unto God, which is your reasonable service. And be not conformed to this world; but be ye transformed by the renewing of your mind, that ye may prove what is that good, and acceptable, and perfect will of God." Such commitment and yieldedness will govern every area of our lives and when we undergo trying circumstances in life, we will prove what is that "good, and acceptable, and perfect will of God."

An illustration of the deepest meaning of this truth of commitment occurred during one of my pastorates. It was during the war. In the church were two families who had sons in the service of their country. One of these families was outstanding in the leadership it gave to the various activities of the church. The family was a "pillar" in the church. The other family was quiet and unassuming—faithful, however, in attendance at the church services. It was not a family that outwardly exhibited its faith by public testimony as did the family prominent in the church. One day tragedy struck in the quiet, unassuming family when the familiar telegram came announcing that their boy had been killed in the line of duty.

As pastor, I was called upon to hold memorial services for the young man. I went out to the farm home prior to the service to ride to the church with the family. Before leaving the house, the father and mother and I went into one of the rooms of the home—apart from the other people—to have a word of prayer. I shall never forget, as I finished my prayer, hearing the quiet, dedicated voice of the mother offering a prayer of thanksgiving to God for the fulfillment of his will in the family's life and in the life of their only child—their beloved son.

I was quite surprised at such a prayer. Having never realized that this family was more than a nominal Christian family, I was totally unprepared for such a prayer. And yet here was a family that was proving, amidst most difficult circumstances, "that good, and acceptable, and perfect will of God."

But imagine my bewilderment when some days later I was visiting in the home of the other family, known for its prominent service to the church. The topic of conversation turned to the tragic death of the only son of the first family. We all expressed our deepest regret and grief. Then as I was concluding my visit, the mother—always so active and prominent in the church—startled me with this statement, "If God takes my son in death, as he did that of my friend, I will hate God all the rest of my life."

Here was a Christian woman—noted for her Christian faith and work—who had not learned the most important lesson for the believer, that of full surrender and commitment to Christ. She had failed to learn the meaning of proving, in daily Christian experience, what is "that good, and acceptable, and perfect will of God."

Commitment to Christ means that the whole man, the total personality, in every area of life must be unreservedly committed to the Spirit's leading. As Paul noted: "That the righteousness of the law might be fulfilled in us, who walk not after the flesh, but after the Spirit" (Romans 8:4). And, as Isaiah puts it: "And thine ears shall hear a word behind thee, saying, This is the way, walk ye in it. . ." (Isaiah 30:21). To such a command the committed man will not hesitate to give obedience.

He Will Be a Chastised Man

The holiness of God makes it imperative, if we desire to lead holy lives, that we submit to the discipline of God's will for our lives. And here, of course, most of us falter and fail. We can take the good things which come our way but we are puzzled by the difficulties we encounter. We are so prone to measure God's blessings in terms of peace and prosperity. We do not recognize that many times his love is most abundantly manifested when we undergo severe chastening and suffering. The writer to the Hebrews says: "For whom the Lord loveth he chasteneth, and scourgeth every son whom he receiveth" (Hebrews 12:6).

We need to learn that there is an inseparable connection between chastisement and holiness. Drawing the analogy between the discipline of our earthly fathers and that of our heavenly Father the writer to the Hebrews notes: "For they verily for a few days chastened us after their own pleasure; but he for our profit, that we might be partakers of his holiness" (Hebrews 12:10). He who would be truly holy in life must learn to adjust to the sufferings and chastisements which God sends his way.

The true way to holiness is not to be found in some minimal definition of sin which includes acts and motivations. Some quote glibly Hebrews 12:14: "Follow peace with all men, and holiness, without which no man shall see the Lord." However, they fail to recognize what has gone before: "Now no chastening for the present seemeth to be joyous, but grievous: Nevertheless afterward it yieldeth the peaceable fruit of righteousness unto them which are exercised thereby. Wherefore lift up the hands which hang down, and the feeble knees; and make straight paths for your feet, lest that which is lame be turned out of the way; but let it rather be healed." To be holy, one must undergo suffering and chastisement. A truly holy life is one lived in the very center of God's will, submissively adjusted to God's disciplining dealings. Paul succinctly states: "Yea, and all that will live godly in Christ Jesus shall suffer persecution" (2 Timothy 3:12).

He Will Be a Communing Man

The life of holiness will be a life of prayer and the man who wants to be a holy man will be a communing man. For the answers to our prayers, according to the Word of God, are proportional to our holiness. Note Isalm 66:18, 19: "If I regard iniquity in my heart, the Lord will not hear me; but verily God hath heard me; he hath attended to the voice of my prayer." Perhaps if some of us are having difficulty securing answers to our prayers we ought to examine our lives.

We need to exercise the unceasing communion with God in prayer. This does not mean necessarily that volume in prayer will gain answers; it means that an attitude and atmosphere of prayer should characterize our lives. For it is contriteness of heart that counts with God: "The Lord is nigh unto them that are of a broken heart; and saveth such as be of a contrite spirit" (Psalm 34:18). James reminds us that the "effectual fervent prayer of a righteous man availeth much" (James 5:16). Prayer, indeed, changes things and men. Our prayer should be: "O, to be like him!"

Therefore, as we conclude our discussion of this most important and fundamental attribute of

God, we need to realize that a proper emphasis upon the holiness of God will give a man a sense of awe in the presence of an absolutely holy God. For God's holiness will reveal his own utter corruption, wickedness, and sin. It will cause him to cry out for divine cleansing and consecration. It will give to God's love the right perspective and show sin to be what it really is—a violation of the holy nature of God. It will call the believer to a life of disciplined, holy living and will cause him in humble submission to God to pray:

> Take my life, and let it be
> Consecrated, Lord, to thee;
> Take my hands, and let them move
> At the impulse of Thy love.
>
> Take my will, and make it Thine,
> It shall be no longer mine;
> Take my heart, it is Thine own;
> It shall be Thy royal throne.
>
> Frances Ridley Havergal

3

THE SOVEREIGNTY OF GOD

Ecclesiastes 7:13, 14

J. Grant Howard, Jr.
Th.D.

Introduction

One of the problems that we face as Christians is that of "spiritual indigestion." As we take in large quantities of truth our spiritual esophagus becomes larger and larger, and our spiritual stomach becomes distended. But our capacity to assimilate truth into our spiritual bloodstream is less than our intake capacity. As a result we suffer from spiritual indigestion. The truth piles up in the pit of our spiritual stomachs. We then tend to measure growth on the basis of how much we have stuffed in rather than how much we have lived out. Thus we can be both overfed and undernourished at the same time. We tend to gauge our spiritual health by that exquisite feeling of spiritual fullness. Then the pressure produced by undigested truth begins to build up. We let others know we have been feasting on the heavenly manna as well as relieve the pressure a bit by what we might classify as a "doctrinal burp"—usually in the form of a Christian cliche that gives the impression we are spiritually "with it." Yet when we come to grips with the truth of the Word of God we find that it is not simply to be known but to be lived, not simply facts to be ingested into our spiritual stomach for storage but to be digested into our total life for use.

Let us look at a passage of Scripture where the writer led by the Spirit of God does just that—he takes a profound doctrine and says, "This ought to touch life." The passage is Ecclesiastes, chapter seven. The early part of this chapter deals with the fact that these people were having problems—struggling with sorrow and mourning in their lives. In verse 11 the writer, Solomon, indicates that what they really need is a healthy dose of divine wisdom. When he refers to wisdom it is what we would call doctrine—spiritual facts that have relevance for our particular situation. He speaks in general terms in verses 11 and 12. He classifies this kind of wisdom as being very profitable; it preserves the lives of those who possess it. In verse 13 he moves from the general to the specific. He shows how you can take a particular part of Gods's wisdom and make it very relevant to your experience. The aspect of wisdom he deals with is the sovereignty of God. Taking this profound truth of God's sovereignty and bringing it down off the shelf and linking it to life, he discusses it under three aspects.

The Reality of the Sovereignty of God

In the first phrase of verse 13 he reminds us of the reality of the sovereignty of God by saying, "Consider the work of God." When he talks about the *work* of God he is referring to something that he had shared with them before. They understood what was meant by "the work of God." It referred to God in charge, God in control, God in command. Put along with this passage Ephesians 1:11 which indicates that God is the one who *works* all things after the counsel of his own will. That is another aspect of God at work which parallels the truth here. Also use Romans 8:28—where all things *work* together for good. When God does things according to his sovereign plan, he is *at work*. This is what Solomon is talking about—the *work* of God—the sovereign plan and purpose and program of God.

He asks them to consider it thoughtfully. Their minds are to be renewed (Romans 12:2) with the careful contemplation of the reality of the sovereign work of God. That is where we must always start—with a knowledge of the truth. We must know the reality of the sovereignty of God. Then we take what we know and relate it to life.

The Relationship of Sovereignty to Life

Having reminded us that the sovereignty of God is a real doctrine, he proceeds to share with us the relationship that the sovereignty of God has to life. He does this first by asking a question in the second part of verse 13. "For who is able to straighten what he has bent?" The question is designed to point up three facts.

First, *what life is like*. It is inconsistent. It is composed of things that are straight and things that are bent. Verse 13 helps us understand that the "straight" is "prosperity," and the "bent" is "adversity." Life for all of us is precisely that way. We have our ups and our downs. We have our smooth spots and our rough spots. We have times of prosperity. We have our times of adversity. That is the reality of life for all of us.

Second, the question is designed to demonstrate *what God can do*. "Who is able to straighten what he has bent?" He can take the straight and make it crooked. He can change the events of our lives from prosperity to adversity. Do you see what is happening? The Scripture is relating the sovereign work of God to the inconsistencies *and* adversities of life! That links the sovereignty of God to the pen that runs out of ink. To the tire that goes flat. To the unexpected, unplanned, and unwanted intrusions. That is what life is like— because that is how God is at work in our lives. He sovereignly programs both the straight and the crooked, the prosperity and adversity.

The question is designed to relate a third fact:

what man can't do. Who is able to straighten what he has bent? The answer is clearly implied—*no one!* In other words, who can reverse the whole process of history and live it over again and do it differently? No one. This is to emphasize the sovereignty of God and the finite limitations of man. Where God has programmed certain things into our life, we do not have the capacity to say "Wait just a minute; let us run that by again. I don't like it like that. Let us do an instant replay with some changes." We can't do that. We don't have the capacity to put the ink back into the pen when it runs out in the middle of a lecture. We don't have the capacity to put the air back into the tire when it goes flat on the freeway. We don't have capacity to make the phone not ring and to cancel the information that came over the phone. It is God's prerogative to reverse and restructure God's program. Solomon is stressing God's capacity to program life for us, and our incapacity to program God.

Following this question in the latter part of verse 13 he gives a set of instructions in the first part of verse 14. In the day of prosperity, be joyful. The first instruction is how to react when things are going well. I suppose he could have left this out. We do not usually have to be told to be happy when things are going well for us. But then again maybe we do need this reminder—maybe we get so used to prosperity that we take it for granted rather than rejoice in it as God's sovereign gift to us. Then he tells us how to react when things are not going so well. "In the day of adversity, consider. . ." We need this instruction. We rejoice when things are going well. But what do we do when things do not go so well?

We get depressed. We get upset. We get discouraged. We get disappointed. But the word of God says that at that point we need to *think!* Think about what? About the fact that God is at work in our lives. That is precisely what the text says. Consider the fact that this God, whom you know to be at work in the world, is at work in your life. He "has made the one (the day of adversity) as well as the other (the day of prosperity)." He programs the experiences of life in such a way that adversity may happen right in the middle of prosperity—without warning! Everything is going along fine and then all of a sudden the unpredicted, unexpected, and often undesired takes place. For the student it may be a pop quiz. For the housewife a stopped-up sink. For the husband an unexpected layoff at the plant. For the motorist a traffic jam on the freeway. For the secretary a headache.

In each case the question is—can you *think* accurately and adequately about the situation? Can you relate the doctrine of the sovereignty of God to your life in those circumstances? A few years ago my wife and I got a sitter for the kids and went to Cannon Beach on the Oregon coast for a weekend. We pulled up in front of the motel and went in to register, looking forward to a pleasure-filled, problem-free weekend. When we gave the clerk our name, she said, "Yes, we were expecting you, and by the way, there was long distance phone call for your wife. Here is the number she is to call." I registered while Audrey went into the office and made the call. She came back a few minutes later and reported in sober, measured tones, "My father just died."

Adversity interjected into prosperity. How do you handle that? Through the tears we had once again the opportunity of bringing our knowledge of the sovereignty of God to bear on our lives right then. We would not have planned the death of an aged, sick father in Toledo, Ohio, for that weekend; but God did, and he is in charge. And he makes no mistakes. His timing is never off. God gave us a few hours of prosperity followed by a few days of adversity—to consider that he had made the one as well as the other. It was a different weekend than we had planned, but it was a good weekend.

When our son, Jim, was a freshman in high school he went out for the track team and soon discovered he had skills in the shot put and discus. At that point I became an avid devotee of high school track meets! One sunny afternoon I went to a meet and watched him throw the discus. On his last throw the discus sailed out beyond the marks of the other competitors. After the measurement Jim came over to me and said, "Dad, I threw it 145 feet. That takes first place and also breaks the school's freshman record!" For his father that was a moment of complete prosperity! I reveled in it as only a proud, grateful and happy father can. In those moments of inner exultation I was anticipating the future—state championships, college scholarships, even the Olympics! I repeat—it was for me a moment of absolute prosperity!

A few minutes later my wife arrived with our

three girls. Excitedly I relayed to them how Jim had won the discus and had also broken the freshman school record. As soon as I finished she said, "That's terrific, but—I've got something to tell you. Dr. Mattson called just before we left the house, to say that the mole he removed from your abdomen was sent to the lab and the report just came back. You've got cancer."

I went from prosperity to adversity. From the heights of happiness to the depths of despair. Without any warning. No advance notice. Who programmed it that way? God did. He made the one (prosperity) as well as the other (adversity). Now it was my challenge to see if I could relate the sovereignty of God to my own life. That was not easy. It is not hard to see God involved in a son that excels in athletics, but it is tough to see God in cancer cells. A few days later I underwent extensive surgery, and to this day there has been no recurrence of the cancer. During those days I found myself coming to grips with sovereignty— not as a theoretical doctrine, not as a doctrine that I studied and taught and preached, but a doctrine that I had to assimilate into my own life. I found the straight and smooth of prosperity had been changed into the rough and rugged of adversity and I had to learn personally to consider these events as God at work in my life. Out of this experience came a deepening commitment that God is in control and that he makes no mistakes. And from this experience also came the questions we all ask. "Why the sudden interruption of prosperity with adversity?" "Why adversity at all?" The latter part of verse 14 tells us why.

The Reason for
Sovereignty in the Life

God programs adversity right next to prosperity for a reason. "So that man may not discover anything that will be after him." To paraphrase it: "So that man doesn't know for sure what's coming next." If we knew when adversity was coming, we would muster all of our human resources to prepare for it and/or avoid it. And the more we developed our skills to handle it on our own, the less we would need God. So God programs life with prosperity and adversity to help us learn to trust him. The just are to live by faith. God provides the context where we have to exercise faith. He helps us put Proverbs 3:5, 6 into operation. To trust in the Lord with all our heart is to acknowledge him in *all* our ways. So there is a sense in which the inconsistencies of life keep us off balance. But when we are off balance we learn to *lean*. And when we are convinced that it is a sovereign God who programs the unbalancing situations into our lives, then we can learn to lean on him for comfort, strength, and wisdom in the midst of those unsettling situations.

Freeways are built with planned curves and hills. Why? To keep motorists alert. When the road is perfectly smooth and perfectly straight, drivers do not pay close attention to their driving, and accidents occur. God is the master traffic engineer of life. He knows that if life for us were straight and smooth we would not remain spiritually alert. We would be tempted to go it alone. So he programs into each life prosperity *and* adversity, often without any warning. Not to keep us guessing, but trusting—trusting in a sovereign God who is in charge of all the details of my life and who programs what's best for me every day.

HOW
BIG
IS
YOUR
GOD?

*H. Crosby
Englizian*
Th.D.

The importance of God to the life of man will not be denied by very many. Diversity of opinion arises, however, as men begin defining their particular god. Scripture tells us, "Though there be those that are called gods" and there are many such, "to us there is but one God, the Father, of whom are all things . . . and one Lord Jesus Christ by whom are all things." Paul then adds (1 Corinthians 8:7), "Howbeit there is not in every man that knowledge."

That man who refuses to accept the God of the Bible is destined to follow a god of his own making; there is but one God. (Others called god are but figments of man's perverted imagination.) When our modern theologians speak of the death of God, they speak of the death of *their* god. What man creates, he can easily dispose of. When man goes about to fashion a god of his own choosing, you may be sure that god will be as good as he who fashioned it: imperfect, imbalanced, arbitrary, and fitted to the mind and desires of its creator, and therefore vain and nonsaving. (See Romans 11:33-36.)

In this text there is an unparalleled characterization of the one, true God. The apostle Paul is not interested in demeaning him, or in robbing him of his personality and deity, or in saying he is passé. Rather he praises him to the extent that language can allow. A correct view of God will always produce this kind of doxology. A correct understanding of the doctrines of grace will ascribe all glory to God. Views of God which are not biblical, views of salvation which attribute its experience by man to the deeds of man, can never produce such a statement.

The book of Romans, especially the first eleven chapters, reveals to man the grace of God in showing us our sinful state, in providing redemption through faith in his Son, in fashioning us who are redeemed according to the likeness of Christ, and in giving us eternal life in a glorified state. It tells us that as the Gentiles came to hear the gospel because of the national rejection of the Jew, so now in the church age many Jews will yet hear the gospel because of a Gentile witness. This is declared in verse 32: "For God hath concluded them all in unbelief, that he might have mercy upon all."

There are a number of triplets in this passage: the knowledge, judgments, and ways of God. Then, there are three questions: one for each of these descriptions. And, finally, in verse 36, God is the source, the mediator or agent, and the end of all things. Let us examine each of these three descriptive characterizations of God and close with the summation in verse 36, which reads: "For of him, and through him, and to him, are all things: to whom be glory forever."

The Knowledge and Wisdom of God

God is rich in knowledge and wisdom and his riches are infinite—deep—or as we sometimes say, he is omniscient. God's knowledge is all-inclusive of everything past, everything present, and everything future. His knowledge is perfect; immediate; i.e., not through experience or development; true and purposive; i.e., always put to a good moral purpose. He knoweth our frame, says the psalmist; he remembereth that we are dust. He knows that being what we are by nature and by choice we are doomed to flounder, and despite our brilliance, to final failure. He knows the end as well as the beginning for he is the first and the last. And through his eternal wisdom he has applied this full knowledge of all things toward his own glorious ends, included within which are the Christian's election and salvation.

Who hath directed the Spirit of the Lord, or being his counselor hath taught him? With whom took he counsel, and who instructed him, and taught him in the path of judgment, and taught him knowledge, and showed to him the way of understanding? (Isaiah 40:13, 14).

Who taught God that which he knows? What school did he attend? Who were his tutors? Being the creator and the preserver of what he has created, providing for every eventuality, hence unperturbed by accident and emergency, including in his universal plan from eternity past all persons, all events, and all things, what remains for him to know? With God there is and there can be no deficiency of knowledge or wisdom for man to supply. And yet the history of the church reveals, a thousand times over, man's attempt to improve God's character and to have him say what he never said and to have him do what he could never do. Man cannot and will not understand God's mind apart from submission to Jesus Christ. It is quite obvious that the only one who can make God known and understood is he alone who has the capacity—God.

The Judgments or Judicial Acts of God

As would be expected of a God who is rich in wisdom and knowledge, his judgments are unsearchable. Is God just? Are his acts always just and fair to all parties concerned? Is his decision to elect some to salvation and not others a just decision? Is God unjust in not saving all men? And yet Romans 9:13 says, "Jacob have I loved; Esau have I hated"; even before these boys were born, God chose to show mercy to one over the other. Was he unjust in this choice?

Justice must proceed on the ground of knowledge. In order for a judge to dispense justice he must know all the facts; to determine what are all the facts, a prosecutor and a defense counsel are employed. The judge, not being omniscient, requires the assistance of counselors to bring to public view all relevant data, to the end that a fair and equitable judgment be made.

But Paul now asks: "Who hath been *his* counselor?" Who has counseled God to give him needed information? What man is there that can inform God of something about which God knows nothing? Since God is perfect in knowledge and wisdom, then it must follow that his judgments are equally perfect. If man is unable to impart any knowledge to God, then he is unable, incapacitated, to question his divinely perfect judgments and decisions.

The human heart being what it is, man is not satisfied to accept God for what he is; his divine nature and character and his works are continually under question—even by some of his children. Someone asks: what kind of a God would send men to hell? Why doesn't God punish the warmongers of the world so the rest of us can live our lives in peace? Why did I have to have parents that never understood me and didn't encourage me to achieve and to get ahead? Why did God permit the life of that sweet, useful Christian to be taken when there are so many evil men who contribute nothing wholesome to society?

Now, I too am a man of the earth, like you, but viewing such questions from a thoroughly committed, biblical point of view, I find that they represent a certain degree of rebellion against God, a partial rejection, at least, of his knowledge and justice. It is really an amazing thing that any man should think himself competent to question any one of God's judgments. In Job 42:2 Job says, "I know that thou canst do everything and that no thought can be withholden from thee; . . . therefore have I uttered that I understood not; things too wonderful for me, which I knew not." He then assumes the proper attitude: "I abhor myself and repent in dust and ashes."

Do you think it proper that a butcher should question the professional doings of a lawyer? A chimney sweep, of a physician? A dogcatcher, of an architect? A ditchdigger, of a chef? Do you think it proper that a man should question God: his motives, judgments, and decisions? Eve questioned God and we know too well the fruit of that disastrous choice. But in Romans 9:20, 21 we read: "Nay but, O man, who art thou that repliest against God? Shall the thing formed say to him that formed it, Why hast thou made me thus? Hath not the potter power over the clay, of the same lump to make one vessel unto honor, and another unto dishonor?" Are we willing to let God be God? Many are not willing and are thus making gods of their own. In the final analysis, of course, irrespective of what we or anyone else might choose to think, God will be what he always has been. Wisdom would dictate that we accept him as we find him, not in our fallible, faltering minds— but as he is, in the Scriptures.

The Ways and Thoughts of God

God's ways are past finding out—untraceable; they cannot be traced or tracked. Isaiah renders the thought: My ways are not your ways. My thoughts are not your thoughts. Man must understand that he is not of the same mold as God. We are among the created; he, the uncreated. The gap between God and man is so vast that the psalmist is led to ask, "What is man that thou art mindful of him . . . and visitest him?" (Psalm 8:4).

Paul now poses his third question: "Who hath first given to him and it shall be recompensed to him again?" (11:35), i.e., what man has ever given something needful to God which gift placed God in man's debt? There is no imperfection in God which man can supply. God is not in man's debt. God has no obligation to man. The opposite is the truth.

The point to be made here is that God is a wholly perfect being; a universal, absolute, and eternal king who has created and controls and possesses all things, yet needing nothing which he has created.

Since God is perfect, it is impossible for any man to impose obligation upon him. Neither piety nor service obligate God. God's ways are free; i.e., he does what he does according to his own good pleasure, wholly undeterred by what we might do for or against him.

Before leaving this point, it might be helpful to add that although God's ways are untraceable, this does not mean he is arbitrary, indecisive, compulsive, or enigmatic. Though God's ways are beyond our ways and though he is incomprehensible and mysterious, his ways are nevertheless bound by his nature. Though we may not understand or comprehend all his acts, we can know that his acts will always be in harmony with his perfect goodness.

The Conclusion To Be Drawn

The riches of his knowledge, his unsearchable judgments, his untraceable ways reveal and extend God's glory from ages past to the eternal ages to come. "For of him, and through him, and to him, are all things: to whom be glory for ever" (vs. 36).

Of him are all things. He is the creator of the heavens and earth (Colossians 1:16). He is the justifier of them who believe.

Through him are all things. He is the mediator and providential agent through whom the divine plan for the world is acted out (1 Corinthians 8:6). He is the sanctifier of those whom he has declared righteous.

To him are all things. All things and all persons are to find their consummation in him (Revelation 4:11). He is the glorifier of those whom he has justified and sanctified. Read Romans 8:30.

All of this he has done according to his own knowledge and wisdom and judgments and ways—independently of us. Is this not good? Yes! Has he not done well? Yes! Then, let us say also that everything else that God is doing is good and above question.

5

GOD, THE GRACIOUS ONE

W. R. Cook
Th.D.

There are those who would have us believe that love is the epitome of the attributes of God, while others just as firmly insist that it is holiness. My suspicions are that both schemes are fraught with danger and set for failure. Love is the attribute of self-communication and when overdrawn tends to magnify immanence at the expense of transcendence. The "love-is-all" advocate tends to sentimentalize life because at best his view of God is pantheized and at worst is pantheistic. On the other hand, holiness is the attribute of separation and distinctiveness. When it is overemphasized, transcendence tends to eclipse immanence. The "holiness-is-all" advocate tends to view life apathetically because his view of God sees him as aloof to the mundane, which is an incipient form of deism.

It would appear, then, that it is folly to try to epitomize God in either of these attributes, or in any other, for that matter. No more can the infinite God be summarized in one of his perfections than he can be comprehended in a simple definition. Biblically oriented wisdom would seem to dictate that we preserve the tension created by the juxtaposition of these admittedly basic perfections. Thus we see a God of holy love and loving holiness.

But what is the secret that enables us to resolve this apparent ambivalence of a God who is at once wholly other and self-communicative? How can our deafened or unattuned ear hear the tones of his truly symphonic nature? Can it be in the majestic attribute of grace, which likewise is in a class apart? Love can be perfectly realized in purely intertrinitarian relationships. Holiness may be true both essentially and ethically by virtue of the simple fact that the Creator is distinct from his creation. Sovereign grace alone can bring the infinitely Holy One to extend his love to those who are a caricature of his image in being both unholy and unloving. Grace is the great interpretive perfection of God. By it God was moved to translate himself into human form in the incarnation, and by it he was moved to translate some among the sons of men into sons of God through the application of the redemptive work of Christ.

The Aspects of Grace

As an aspect of God's goodness, grace is closely related to his love and mercy. Love is that in God which eternally moves him to self-communication, while grace more narrowly defines an aspect of that active love in relation to the undeserving. It differs from mercy as a positive differs from a negative. Mercy contemplates man in his misery and provides relief. Grace discovers man under wrath and replaces it with favor.

Also, there is some similarity between grace and omnipotence in that grace effects moral ends that are otherwise impossible of realization. The difference is that omnipotence is an unrestricted attribute of sovereignty related to will, while grace is a specific aspect of goodness relating in its exercise to God's moral creatures.

What, then, is the grace concerning which we speak? It is that intrinsic quality of God's character by which he is constituted freely and spontaneously favorable in his disposition and actions. It is, first of all, essential and therefore inseparably related to every other quality of his character, every perfection of his person, and every aspect of his decree. Consequently, because this grace in God is active and outgoing it seeks an object upon which it can be centered apart from that object's merit or request. Thus, while at its source grace is God's favorable disposition, it *becomes* acts of favor bestowed on the undeserving, indeed on those who deserve the very opposite, without any relation to obligation.

The Analysis of Grace
Grace in God

This is the quality of the divine essence from which springs all the spontaneous favor which God bestows on man (1 Peter 5:10; Romans 5:15; 2 Corinthians 8:9; 2 Thessalonians 1:12).

—It is necessary: it relates to a quality of essence rather than to an act of will.
—It is subjective: it is true of God as a subject prior to and apart from his creatures.
—It is intrinsic: it is basically ontological rather than economical.
—It is essential: it is inseparably related to the divine nature and therefore pervades every perfection of his person and every aspect of his decree.

Grace from God

This is the free act of God, tempered by justice and holiness, in spontaneously bestowing favor upon undeserving and condemned mankind without any relation to reciprocal obligation (Romans 3:24; 11:5, 6; Ephesians 2:8, 9; Titus 2:11; 3:7).

—It is free: it is an act of the divine will contingent upon nothing external to the divine being.
—It is objective: it devolves upon real objects of his creative work, namely, mankind.
—It is spontaneous: it neither arises because sought after nor is prompted by anything outside the one who exercises it;

although it meets our need it does not
arise out of need.

—It is not capricious: it is a deliberate, pre-
meditated, intelligent, and wise act.

—It is undeserved: it does not consider the
unworthiness of the receiver as an ob-
stacle, it is not hindered by sin, and it is
not conditioned by works.

—It is bestowed: it is of the character of "gift"
and thus is without any relation to reciprocal obligation.

The Application of Grace

But grace is not fully nor properly perceived if it
is seen only as being *in* God or *from* God. It must
also be viewed in its effects as received by and its
evidences as manifested through the believer. To
put it another way, there is not only God's grace
but also the Christian's grace. Surely there is a line
of continuity to be established between the two but
it is important to keep them distinct.

This facet of truth is reinforced in Scripture by
every passage which teaches us regarding our
proper duty to glorify God. He is glorified in every
display of his ineffable character. The believer is
privileged to give evidence of his great God both in
what he is (John 17:10) and in what he does
(1 Corinthians 10:31). One of the perfections of
God to be thus demonstrated is grace.

First, in this connection, we must consider grace
in its effects as received by the Christian.

—We are saved by grace and thus grace becomes the source of our richly endowed

life (Ephesians 2:8, 9; 2 Corinthians 8:9).
—We stand in grace and thus grace is the source of our safety and security (Romans 5:2).
—God's blessings are bestowed in grace and thus grace is the source of our good works (service) (2 Corinthians 9:8; cf. Ephesians 2:10).
—Grace is the sphere of Christian living and thus is the source of our sustenance and growth (John 1:16; 2 Peter 3:18) of our sufficiency and strength (2 Corinthians 12:9; Hebrews 4:16).
—Grace is our teacher and thus the source of a holy walk in daily life (Titus 2:11-13).

Now, because of this all-encompassing work of grace and the resultant perfect standing we have in Christ (see Hebrews 10:10, 14) the obligation to gain merit is removed as a legitimate motive in the Christian life. The question is not: "What can I do to maintain favor?" but, "How should I walk so as to manifest favor (grace)?" What is the proper response to grace? Partial answer to this question may be found in an illustration from daily life. When I leave home each day to go to my office I kiss my wife goodbye. Why? Because it is merely a habit or the nice thing to do? No. Because I am afraid she will not love me if I do not? No. Rather, it is a spontaneous response of love to love. It is not to maintain favor with her but because I have favor with her and she with me. So it should be with the child of God and his Heavenly Father.

There are two etymologically and ideologically cognate terms which give us further answer to this question. The New Testament term for grace may also, on occasion, mean either "gracious" or "grateful." Thus grace in the Christian will manifest itself in graciousness (bestowal of favor and/or beauty of character) and gratitude. These graces ought not to be manifested simply because we owe them to him but as the spontaneous expression of an unfettered spirit.

Graciousness will take varied forms:

—Since the riches of grace have become our wealth (Ephesians 1:6; 2:6, 7) benevolence should attend our every action.

—Since the melody of grace has become our song (Colossians 3:16) a buoyant spirit should characterize our attitudes.

—Since the words of grace have become our conversation (Colossians 4:6) heaven's wisdom should punctuate our speech.

—Since the gifts of grace have become our stewardship (1 Peter 4:10, 11) glory to God should be the issue of our service.

—Since the gospel of grace is our message (1 Corinthians 15:3-11) the edification of the saints and the salvation of the lost will be the result of its enunciation.

Finally, an aspect of Christian grace is the gratefulness we should express. Two examples from Scripture must suffice as reminders of the kinds of things for which we should express thanks (grace):

—for the conquest of death; 1 Corinthians 15:54-57, "Thanks be to God, which giveth us the victory through our Lord Jesus Christ."

This is not merely a deliverance from death but a deliverance through it. It is not merely victory over the horror of death but over the power of death for its sting is removed by the assurance of resurrection. It is thus the introductory step in incorruptibility, immortality, and glorification. "Therefore, my beloved brethren, be ye steadfast, unmoveable, always abounding in the work of the Lord, forasmuch as ye know that your labor is not in vain in the Lord" (v. 58).

—for a conquered and fragrant life; 2 Corinthians 2:14, "Now thanks be unto God, which always causeth us to triumph in Christ, and maketh manifest the savor of his knowledge by us in every place."

—the two participles "leading in triumph" and "making manifest" are very closely related grammatically. It must not be missed that the fragrance of the knowledge of God in Christ is only made manifest as we accept the place of the conquered.

Thus grace has come full circle. Grace *in* God has become grace *from* God. Grace from God has become grace *in* the Christian. This, in turn, has become grace *from* the Christian in the form of graciousness to his fellows and gratefulness to God.

6

THE LONGSUFFERING OF GOD

Stanley E. Ellisen
Th.D.

The Bible is God's revelation of himself to men. It is a revelation of his person, his program, and his principles. To know *God* is the highest level of knowledge. To study his creation is to think great thoughts, to be sure; but to study about the Creator *himself* is far more expansive. It takes us infinitely beyond human studies. And, interestingly, when we climb to this high level of knowledge, many of our common, perplexing problems in life evaporate. Job, for example, once sat on an ash heap outside the city of Uz in the garbage dump; he had a lot of problems that overwhelmed him. But when God finally came to him, he didn't answer any of his problems in logical, forthright answers. All he did was to give Job a glimpse of the Almighty himself and his "daily chores." When he saw God, all of his problems disappeared; he forgot about them in the presence of the Person of God. And I think this is also essential for us. We need to know God; we need to be problem-conscious, certainly; but we need to recognize that many of our problems will disappear if we have a proper concentration on the person and principles of God. Our orientation, in other words, should be around the person of God, rather than around the problems of men. The world and its problems will then come into proper perspective as we first bring God into focus in our thinking.

I emphasize this, because the study of the attributes of God is sometimes thought of as a doctrinal subject, without very much practical import. We need to recognize, on the contrary, that it is indeed intensely practical to study the person and attributes of our God.

This subject of the longsuffering of God is not one that is greatly expounded today. To see it in its proper perspective, we shall consider first its nature, then its purpose, and finally its implications.

The Nature of God's Longsuffering

What specifically is meant by God's longsuffering? How does this feature of his being relate to his nature? To discern its special significance, we should recall that the three supreme attributes of

God are his *truth*, his *holiness*, and his *love*. These various aspects of his nature at times appear somewhat in conflict, but they are not. The three really complement each other and coalesce in his nature. Let's briefly review them.

God's truth, first of all, is the consistency or invariableness of his nature. He cannot lie and is absolutely trustworthy in all he says or does. This expresses the immutability of his character in all his pronouncements. All that he promises will be fulfilled without fail.

God's holiness relates to his truth but is broader in extending his immutability to his whole being. It is often thought of as the purity of his character. This concept of purity, however, does not just mean that God is clean or free from impurities. That, of course, is true, but it misses the real meaning of his "purity" or holiness. Maybe we can illustrate it by considering the designation "pure" that is put on a can of produce in the grocery store. What is meant when you pick up a can of apple juice and it says "pure apple juice"? Does it mean that the apple juice is clean, or that it hasn't been contaminated? No! That is taken for granted in its being offered for sale. "Pure" simply means that it contains *apple juice* and *only apple juice*. It has no water mixed with it; it is strictly apple juice, and nothing but apple juice.

Now, that's what is meant by the purity or holiness of God. He is God, he is all God, and he is nothing but God. We sometimes refer to it as his "wholeness," which perhaps is not far from the mark. He does not compromise with anything contrary to his nature. Sin can have no part in the nature of God. That is his holiness.

The third aspect of his nature is his love. As his holiness is the purity or *preservation* of his nature, so his love is the *communication* of his nature. Now, it's interesting that the two words "holiness" and "love" (*haggios* and *agape*) come from similar roots. Similarly, although they emphasize two different aspects of his being, they both speak of his nature. There is no conflict between these aspects of God's nature, and there never was even a "seeming conflict" until the entrance of sin. When sin entered, however, it set up something of a tension, humanly speaking, between itself and the holiness of God. Sin appeared to be a challenge to God's very nature. In the fall of man, God's creatures believed a lie in conflict with *God's truth*, thus deserving wrath according to *God's holiness*, and, in turn, introduced something of a frustration of *his love*. In other words, it was difficult for God to express his love towards those who deserved his wrath. Being immutable, God could not change his nature or adjust it to accommodate sin. Rather, he interposed something new: his grace. And his grace is that aspect of his love which is shown to people who deserve the exact opposite. In this sense, it is really a special aspect or expression of his love.

Thus God expressed himself in two ways at the entrance of sin. With respect to his love, he showed mercy; with respect to his holiness, he showed longsuffering. To vessels of mercy, he showed mercy; to vessels of wrath, longsuffering.

The point we would stress here is that God's longsuffering relates primarily to his wrath (that is, the delay of his wrath), rather than to his love. To see this I would like us to look at two verses which speak of the longsuffering of God. In Exodus 34:6 and 7, the first reference to God's longsuffering is found. The term actually is used only about sixteen times in the whole Bible: four times in the Old Testament (as *erech aph*), and twelve times in the New Testament. Only five of the New Testament references, however, speak of God's longsuffering. Thus concerning God, it is used four times in the Old Testament and five in the New Testament.

To see its significance, we should look at its first reference in Exodus 34. Recall with me the context. Israel had just been given a revelation of God—a revelation of his holiness—and almost immediately they sinned in the calf-worship of national idolatry. Because of this, they all deserved to die. Instead of that judgment, God acceded to Moses and declared in Exodus 34:6: "The Lord, The Lord God, merciful and gracious, longsuffering, and abundant in goodness and truth." In identifying himself thus, did he mean that he was passing over their sin and forgetting his outraged holiness? Not at all. They obviously deserved wrath and death as a part of the Mosaic code that God had just given Moses in the Mount. But he introduced another aspect of his nature by saying in verse seven: "Keeping mercy for thousands, forgiving iniquity, transgression, and sin: that will by no means clear the guilty." In other words, God here declared that although he was postponing his wrath, he had not forgotten their sin. His "longsuffering," in other words, was interposed to postpone his wrath.

This, then, is the first reference in the Bible to this term, and it is appealed to three times later—once by Moses again in Numbers 14, when Israel again had sinned; once by David in Psalm 86; and once by Jeremiah in Jeremiah 15. Each of these is used of God when his people had broken his law and deserved judgment. Each time his longsuffering intervened to delay the application of his wrath, but not to eliminate it. By contrast, it is interesting to notice that God's *mercy* is said to endure *forever*—but not his longsuffering. By the very nature of the case (the nature of the term "longsuffering"), it is not to continue forever. It is simply an interposition of divine restraint, a delay of his wrath to accomplish other purposes. It was not an annullment of that wrath.

Reflecting a bit on our generation, it appears that this clarification of God's longsuffering is quite significant. We live in a day in which the concept of God's wrath and holiness has been watered down by emphasizing some kind of a gushy, sentimental concept of love. His love and his holiness, supposedly, are in a conflict; but, in the end, God's love is going to prevail and triumph over his judgment, and all the strays are going to be welcomed back into the Father's house. Well, I'll tell you something: God's love is going to triumph, and gloriously, but not at the expense of his holiness. It will not prevail by violating another aspect of his being. He is not going to overhaul his nature because of the circumstance of sin. And I think that this will become clear as we notice further the *purpose* of God's longsuffering.

The Purpose of God's Longsuffering

We naturally ask what God's purpose is in showing longsuffering to sinners. Negatively, it should be noted that its purpose is not to compromise with sin as allowing some kind of an "indulgence." It is not some kind of an emotional sympathy which wells up in God and makes his wrath capitulate in the face of human sorrow. God does not overlook sin, but rather looks beyond it. He looks beyond to the greater results and benefits which will accrue through his further work. This is especially noted by Paul in Romans 9:22 where he says: "What if God, willing to show his wrath and to make his power known, endured with much longsuffering the vessels of wrath fitted to destruction, and that he might make known the riches of his glory on the vessels of mercy. . . ?"

Notice that the *first of these benefits* is the salvation of the "vessels of mercy." With the interposition of God's longsuffering, God seeks to salvage and conform to his own image the vessels that receive his mercy. While he has not forgotten sin, he postpones its judgment while he saves those that respond, called the vessels of mercy. This salvaging operation then is the first purpose in God's interposing his longsuffering and delaying his wrath.

A second purpose, and perhaps the primary one, is the greater glory to God that is to result through the introduction of his longsuffering toward us. As we read in Romans 9:22, the Lord endured with the vessels of wrath that he might make known the riches of his glory. The point is that these vessels of mercy will make a contribution to his glory. They will result in glory, not only for us, but primarily for God. The enormous investment which God had made in us—his capital investment in sinners—is going to produce many hundred-fold. God is a wise investor. We should not forget that the most important purpose of God's long-suffering is to increase and intensify the glory of God. And what could be more important than his glory!

A final purpose of God's longsuffering is that this quality of our God—his longsuffering—might be implanted in us, the vessels of mercy. As believers, we have a high calling and a great future. We are called to rule with God, to judge and put down evil with great power. That, however, is not our commission as a Church today. Rather, we are told to "not recompense to man evil for evil." Vengeance and wrath belong to God, not to us. We live in the recognition that a day is coming when God is going to settle all accounts, and therefore, when we are sinned against, we rest our case with God. He will one day right all wrongs. Though he is long-suffering with sinners today, he hasn't forgotten their wicked ways. We should likewise share that attitude of longsuffering concerning evil in view of the fact that our God will one day settle all accounts.

The Implications of God's Longsuffering

Finally it should be noted that there are several implications of a practical nature that follow from God's longsuffering. For the world, the absence of

God's wrath on sin seems to suggest that either there is no God (no one seems to be judging sin), or that God's holiness and wrath are softening. In that case, he appears to have finally come to a recognition that he has got to compromise his holiness, and is planning some kind of a general amnesty. Many people imagine this. As Ecclesiastes 8:11 says: "Because sentence against an evil work is not executed speedily, therefore the hearts of the sons of men is fully set in them to do evil." Because God does not judge sin immediately, they imagine he has perhaps grown used to sin and is softening in his attitude towards it. Let me say that if it is a horrible mistake to creep up on a sleeping lion and tickle him under the chin, it is far more dangerous and tragic to presume on the mercy and longsuffering of God. It is said that some years ago Mr. Moody was walking the streets of Chicago and came upon an atheist who stood on the corner, ranting and raving against the idea of God. As Moody listened, the atheist took out his watch and said, "I'll give God, if there is a God, sixty seconds to knock me on the ground." This was too much for Mr. Moody who was a man of considerable proportions. He took off his coat, went up to that fellow, and knocked him to the ground. Then he said to him, "Never ask God to do something that his humble servant can mighty well take care of." Well, if this story is true, probably Mr. Moody was out of place here; but he had a point. How easy it is for the world to misunderstand God's longsuffering. He is not today in the business of striking down sinners, but saving them.

You have perhaps heard the story of the Christian farmer who got into a contest with his neighbor who was an atheist. One day the atheist made a proposition to him and said: "I'll tell you what; you plant your crops this spring and work your field six days a week, taking off every Sunday. I'll plant and work mine seven days a week, including Sunday. Then we'll see who gets the best crop and who is right." So the Christian farmer said, "Fine," and they went to farming. Then in October, after the crops were all gathered in, the atheist farmer came around to check up. Looking over their crops they agreed that, sure enough, the atheist had a considerable better harvest than the Christian farmer. With something of a sneer the atheist said, "Well, what do you say now?" Then the Christian farmer responded with what has to be a classic reply. He simply reminded him: "God doesn't settle all his accounts in October."

I think this is one of the mistakes many people are making today with respect to God's longsuffering. Since God showers rain and sunshine on saints and sinners alike, they imagine that this grace and longsuffering mean he has forgotten sin. What a tragic mistake; longsuffering only means a postponement of wrath. And this delay, if anything, will intensify the final application of that wrath. Though the world today is basking in peace and prosperity, tenuous though it is, it should not be misinterpreted. Because God does not now strike out of the sky at sin, the world tends to sneer: "Where is the God of Elijah? Where is the God of the Bible? Why does he not do something if he does not like what we are doing?" The natural tendency of the world is to go about their sinning and ignore God for his lack of shouting from the sky. God's longsuffering, we emphasize, is meant to remind us that we live today in the lull before the storm: but his pent-up wrath is not going to be delayed forever. "My Spirit shall not always strive with men," God said. The final book of the Bible devotes most of its pages to an elucidation of God's coming judgment as his longsuffering comes to an end.

These are not soothing thoughts, admittedly, but are most essential in considering the character of God and the salvation he offers. His longsuffering has not annulled his judgment. I am reminded of a young preacher who was trying to get up a sermon for the following Sunday, but had trouble getting an inspiration. Finally, on Saturday afternoon, getting frantic, he decided to take a drive around town to get his theological adrenalin flowing. As he and his wife rode through town, they came around a corner and suddenly saw a house on fire. Stopping, they saw a man come running out with one child and, laying it on the ground, dash back into the flames for the others. The sight of this man saving his family from death really inspired the preacher. Reflecting on it, he thought it would be a tremendous illustration around which to build a sermon. So, on Sunday morning he got up to preach and told the story as an illustration. He described how the man came running out of the house with one child after another and finally with his wife, nearly dropping in exhaustion. Well, the preacher used the illustration and tried to apply it, but somehow it went over like a lead balloon. The people just did not seem to catch on and so he finally closed the service. On his way home he said to his wife: "You know, I can't understand why there seemed to be so little response by the people—they didn't seem to get the point I was making."

"Well," his wife said in understanding, wifely fashion, "it was a fine story and a good application; but you know, John , you forgot to tell them one thing."

"What was that?" he asked.

"You forgot to tell them that the house was on fire."

I wonder if that is the mistake much of our gospel preaching is making today. Are we leaving out the gospel's announcement of God's wrath? Does the world really know the "house is on fire"?

This subject on God's longsuffering is a reminder of the holiness and immutability of God. His wrath against sin has not abated. Sin is as repugnant to God as it ever was. Before his wrath falls on an unrepentant world, however, he has interposed his longsuffering while he salvages out of the world all those who will respond to his offer of mercy. That offer is yet being made to men today. What a privilege it is to be recipients of his grace and to be a part of that redeemed group who will magnify the glory of God, and will, in fact, be a part of that glory.

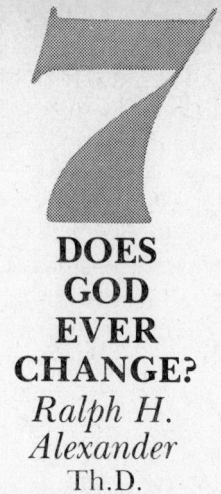

DOES GOD EVER CHANGE?

Ralph H.
Alexander
Th.D.

Approximately 4000 years ago, an almighty and loving God brought a people out of bondage in Egypt. Following that event they rejoiced and praised God. However, three days later these same people found themselves asking God where they might find a drink of water. Two thousand years later, a group of twelve disciples saw this same omnipotent God, Jesus Christ, perform a miracle by feeding five thousand people. Yet not long after that miracle these same disciples asked him how four thousand people might be fed.

Regrettably, this attitude toward God has pervaded history. It is very prevalent today. Undoubtedly, many of us have probably responded in the same manner. We have seen God work miraculously in our lives in the past. Yet now we question whether God could ever work in those ways in our lives again. Some of the things that are going on in our lives are causing us to wonder if God is still the same as he used to be. Does he still work in the same way? Though we would not want to say it outwardly, inwardly we are really asking, "Has God changed?"

The Revelation of God's Unchangeability

This is the same type of situation that Malachi confronted in his day. He related how God reasoned together with the people of Israel concerning his character. In that day they had begun to fall away from following after the ways of God. When Israel did not follow God's ways exactly, they began wondering why God did not respond in the way that they thought he should or in the way that they had heard that God acted in the past. But when they saw that God was not responding in the way that they had expected, they began to become haughty and continued to do more things contrary to God's ways. It was an endless cycle.

It is at this juncture that Malachi confronted the people of Israel. The situation is succinctly summarized in Malachi 2:17. Malachi declared, "You have wearied the Lord with your words. Yet you say, 'How have we wearied him?' In that you say,

'Everyone who does evil is good in the sight of the Lord, and he delights in them' or, 'Where is the God of justice?' " What they were actually saying is, "From our experience and from what we see happening within our own lives, it appears rather evident to us that God does not operate in the same way he did in the past. It seems to us now that God delights in those who do evil. That must be good to God. It just goes to show that God is not just anymore. Where is the God of justice?"

At this point in the argument God himself stepped in and reasoned with Israel concerning the fact that he *never* changes. Never! Israel was saying that God delighted in evil, yet the Word of God in Psalm 5:4 states, "Thou art *not* a God who takes pleasure in wickedness. No evil dwells with thee." Had God changed? The writer of Proverbs in chapter 12, verse 2 said, "A good man will obtain favor from the Lord, but he will condemn a man who devises evil." Had God changed? Israel obviously thought that he had. Therefore, God, in his marvelous grace, sat down, so to speak, and reasoned with the people of Israel. He wanted them to know that they could always rely upon the character of God and his ways, because he *never* changes. Notice how God replied to them, " 'Behold, I am going to send my messenger, and he will clear the way before me. And the Lord, whom you seek, will suddenly come to his temple; and the messenger of the covenant, in whom you delight, behold, he is coming,' says the Lord of Hosts" (Malachi 3:1). Now that seemed like a strange way to begin, yet God was only saying: "I am *still* just! I promised to you, Israel, back in the time of Isaiah (chapter 40), that I would send a forerunner before the coming of the Messiah. That will *still* happen! And when Messiah comes, he will exercise his justice which you think has passed away. No one will be able to endure it. He will judge as a refining fire (v. 2) just as Isaiah said (Isaiah 48). He will cleanse Israel just as God said through the prophet Ezekiel (Ezekiel 36). The result will be that the Levitical priests will bring righteous offerings as Ezekiel declared in his latter chapters (Ezekiel 40–48). In fact, Messiah will be quick as a witness in judgment against sorcerers, adulterers, those who swear falsely, those who extort wages and exploit orphans and widows, and those who thrust aside the stranger. Why? Because in each one of these cases I prohibited such acts in the Mosaic Covenant. You see, I will *still* do what I said I would do." Then the Lord stated the basic thrust of his argument in verse 6, "For I, the Lord, do not change!" "That is why I will continue to be a God of justice, though you do not believe me because of your disobedience."

The Relevance of God's Unchangeability

The issue is very relevant to us. When we disobey God's ways and take the liberty to alter the ways in which man is to respond to God, we are really saying that we want to change God and we want him to be different. Then we may do what *we* want. When God declared that he did not change, he was telling us that his attributes are not alterable. We must also remember that the character of God and the nature of his revelation are intrinsically related. If we say that the Word of God changes, then we are also saying that God changes. Israel was saying, "It does not seem as if God is operating in the same manner. What God used to say and what our experience now dictates seem to be in conflict."

This attitude is very common in our society today. We want to live by experience, and therefore we unconsciously are saying that God must change, or that he already has changed, because we do not see him doing what we think he ought to do. Yet it never enters our mind that we are not following his unchanging ways. God has not changed; we have!

The Lord continued his argument by saying, "Now let me just give you some further illustrations, Israel, that I do not change." The argument followed in Malachi 3:6b: "Therefore you, O sons of Jacob, are not consumed." Why not? Because the covenant promise of God is unchanging and eternal. God promised in the Abrahamic covenant that Israel would be an eternal people; he would give them a land that was everlasting. If Israel were to be consumed, then God has indeed changed. God would no longer be faithful; he would no longer be the God who keeps his promise. Israel responded, "You mean that we are not going to be consumed even though our fathers have turned away from the *stipulations* of your word?" (compare verse 7). The Lord replied, "That's right!"

But this brings up another unchanging principle: God's invitation to Israel never changes! "Return to me, and I will return to you, says the Lord of hosts" (Malachi 3:7b). This invitation is not new, however, for Moses charged Israel in the Sinai covenant which God made with Israel as follows:

> And you return to the Lord your God and obey him, you and your sons, with all your heart and soul according to all that I commanded you today. Then the Lord your God will restore you from captivity, and have compassion on you, and will gather you again from all the peoples where the Lord your God has scattered you (Deuteronomy 30:2, 3).

That invitation has not changed, O Israel! God wanted Israel to return to him, and if she returned to him, he would return to her. This immediately raised a question in the mind of Israel. "How shall we return?" (verse 7c). God responded that Israel should return to him in the very same way she always has, for God's ways do not change! The Lord illustrates: "Israel, in this day you have failed to provide properly for your priests. The Law instructed you to bring the tithes and the contributions to the temple of God in order that there might be provision for the tribe of Levi, which has no land of its own on which to grow their own food. But, Israel, you have not done this. You have robbed God of these provisions. You have failed to do this, Israel, and as a result, you are right now being cursed." Why? Because God promised Israel would be cursed if she failed to provide for the priests. In the cursing and blessing formula of the Mosaic covenant (Deuteronomy 27–28) God declared that if Israel obeyed these stipulations, he would pour out blessing, but if she disobeyed, she would be cursed. Those who did not confirm the words of this Law by doing them would be cursed (Deuteronomy 27:26). Therefore, in Malachi's day God was simply doing what he said he would do in the Mosaic covenant: curse Israel! God had not changed! However, the solution to the cursing had not changed either. If Israel wanted to know how to return to God, she could start by doing God's ways: bring the tithes into the storehouse. In fact, God said, "Put me to the test." "Test me now in this . . . if I will not open for you the windows of heaven, and pour out for you a blessing (of rain) until there is no more need" (Malachi 3:10b). I will destroy those who would destroy the produce of your land.

Malachi 3:10 is a very interesting verse. This is the only place in Scripture where men are commanded to test God. There are many statements in the rest of Scripture that say, "Do not test God." However, we must see the distinction and the context of each. The context here argues that Israel should put God's ways to the test and see if they do not work. "Try me," says God, "and find out that my ways have not changed! Find out that I still respond today as I did in the past! Go right ahead, try it and see if it does not work!" Now there is a big difference between this testing of God's promises and the testing of God which we often like to do. Men like to say, "Now God, you just do it our way, and if you do not do it our way, then there is something wrong with you." Or, "God, we are going to check to see if you meant what you said. We want to see if we can get away with doing wrong." It surely looked as if that was what Israel was doing—and seeming to get away with it. But God said, "No! That is not what I am saying. On the contrary, I challenge Israel to put my character and my ways to the test, for she will find that my character and my ways *never* change! What I say I will do, I will do!"

God gives a second illustration in verses 13-15. "Your words have been arrogant against me, says the Lord." And Israel said, "Well, how?" That is so much like us, isn't it? The Lord tells us that we have been obstinate and have not followed his ways, and yet we tend to go around saying, "Well, how?" The Lord told Israel that he would tell her. "Look, you say it is worthless to serve God" (cf. verse 14a). Of course the Mosaic covenant said that the one who serves God will be blessed and that serving God is for the individual's own good. But we thought God had changed, and therefore, if we served God, it would be worthless. Then we also said, "What do we get out of keeping God's charge?" (compare verse 14b). (This is often the concern of our day—what do *we* get out of every situation?) Israel was not following God's ways, and therefore, there was no profit. However, the circular reasoning then caused Israel to say, "Well, what's the use?" "It seems to us," says Israel, "that the arrogant and the insolent are really the ones who are blessed. In fact you know something, God? Those who are doing wickedness are testing you and getting away with it. You mean to tell us,

God, that in light of all this which we have experienced, you expect us to believe that you are the same God who spoke to Moses? You're kidding! You've obviously changed! Our experience tells us so." This is exactly the way we respond.

The Results of God's Unchangeability

God replied, "Oh, just a moment. Let me show you that I have not changed." He then declared, "Then those who feared the Lord spoke to one another, and the Lord gave attention and heard it." "Israel, the day of the Lord is coming. God will do what he said he would do. You may be as arrogant as you like and think that I will do nothing. You might think that people are escaping who are insolent. But let me tell you something, Israel. When I do come, here are some things that will happen.

"First, I will hear and listen to those who fear me." That never changes. One can always talk to God and know that God always hears and listens attentively. God will mark those people in a memorial book for that future day, just as Daniel declared in Daniel 12. Everyone whose name is listed in the book will be spared in the time of trouble. God said it in Daniel, and it is still true.

Second, on that day the Lord will make up a special possession of his own, the very people of Israel, as God previously declared in Exodus 19:5. But only those who feared the Lord will be part of that "possession"—not the arrogant. In fact, when the Lord returns, there will be a great distinction between the righteous, those serving God, and the wicked, those who are not serving God. The wicked will be like stubble in a burning furnace, but those who fear God will see the Son of Righteousness rise and shine upon them with healing, and they will trample down the wicked. Every one of these promises is previously stated in God's revelation.

It is fascinating that God concludes the Old Testament with a statement of his immutability or unchangeability. He charges Israel to remember the law of Moses. Why? Because God wants Israel to know that his previously revealed ways are still his ways. They have not changed! In addition God wants Israel to remember that a forerunner *will* come, and that has not changed either. God will be as immutable in the future as he is right now, for he *never* changes.

Only we know what our situation is. Only we know whether we think that God is not providing for us today as he provided before. Perhaps we have felt that God called us to a ministry without any question, but we now wonder if God is going to provide for that ministry for which we thought he called us. Remember, God does not change! If God called us to a ministry, he has a place for us. Test God! Try his character! Test his ways, and see if they are not true! As the writer of Hebrews reminds us, "Remember those who led you, who spoke the Word of God to you, and consider the outcome of their way of life, imitate their faith. Jesus Christ is the same yesterday and today, yes and forever" (Hebrews 13:7, 8).

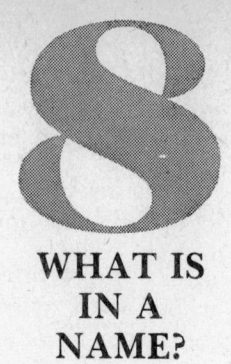

WHAT IS
IN A
NAME?

*Ronald Barclay
Allen*
Th.D.

> What's in a name? that which we call a rose
> By any other name would smell as sweet.

In these words, to which we have become somewhat accustomed and calloused because of their
frequent repetition, the Immortal Bard has asked
a profound question: What in fact is *in* a name?
Act II, Scene II, of *Romeo and Juliet* is one of the
most well known scenes in all drama. When the
young maiden mused from her balcony, "O
Romeo, Romeo! Wherefore art thou Romeo?" she
was not asking *where* he was, but *why* he was *Romeo*.
This is made clear in the following lines:

Deny thy father and refuse thy name;
Or, if thou wilt not, be but sworn my love,
and I'll no longer be a Capulet.

Not yet aware that her lover with the forbidden name was attending her soliloquy, Juliet continued:

'Tis but thy name that is my enemy;
Thou art thyself, though not a Montague.
What's Montague? it is not hand, nor foot,
Nor arm, nor face, nor any other part
Belonging to a man. O, be some other name!
What's in a name? that which we call a rose
By any other name would smell as sweet,
So Romeo would, were he not Romeo call'd,
Retain that dear perfection which he owes
without that title. Romeo, doff thy name,
And for that name which is no part of thee
Take all myself.

Unfortunately, for Romeo (and Juliet), his name was and remained part of him. The tragedy reached its bitter climax in death and despair because of that very fact.

What *is* in a name? In our own culture all names have their meanings, but because of the many languages from which our name-stock is taken, the meanings usually have to be searched out in books designed for expectant parents. It is not the meaning that is paramount, however, in our culture. Rather, usually we give our children names that "sound nice," or that honor a relative or friend. My two boys, for example, were named in honor of two beloved seminary professors. My wife and I chose our daughter's name because we thought it lovely, as we found her to be. Now, *we* know the meanings of their names, and we have taught *them* these meanings as positive personality goals. Others would not know the meanings, however, unless they were to check.

It is in our fuzziness concerning the meaning of names that we are reminded of our great cultural distance from the Old Testament world. For in the world of Abraham, David, and Isaiah, names were common nouns and verbs from the living language and their meanings were transparent. The meaning of a name was in fact the reason for that name being used. L. Köhler has explained that "it is the prevailing view among the Hebrews that names have meaning; they 'speak'" (Ludwig Köhler, *Hebrew Man*, trans. by Peter R. Ackroyd, p. 55). More fully, P.. van Imschoot (Paul van Imschoot, *Theology of the Old Testament*, I. God, trans. by Kathryn Sullivan and Fidelis Buck, p. 35.) wrote,

> In the eyes of the ancients the name was not a simple label distinguishing one individual from his kinsmen. It is an integrating part of the person; what has no name is, so to speak, non-existent. . . . Moreover, the name is supposed to correspond to the essence of the object, and consequently reveals it.

When the interpreter is able to determine the meaning of an Old Testament name, he often finds how very fitting that name is in the role the individual has in a given account. In the Book of Ruth, for example, each name fits so perfectly the role of each character, that the reader finds the story-line advanced considerably by understanding these terms (this is developed in "Notes on the Theology of the Book of Ruth," by Ronald B. Allen, classroom printing for OT 104, Western Baptist Seminary, 1975).

Names in the Old Testament have a particular enchantment to the careful reader. Not all of the Old Testament names are understood today, of course, but where the meaning is clear the names of the characters of Scripture are helpful. Some are humorous, as in the case of Nabal ("fool"). Nabal's life was spared when David's rash vengeance was assuaged by the beauty and tact of Nabal's wife, Abigail, as she joked: "Nabal is his name and folly is with him" (1 Samuel 25:25). From "the fool," she reminded David, what should one expect but folly!

Names in the Old Testament were so filled with meaning that surprisingly often the writers of Scripture deliberately corrupted the pronunciation (and thus the meaning) of the names of pagan gods and their devotees. Examples include Balaam, Jezebel, Ishbosheth, and Baal-zebub.

Had Juliet lived in Jerusalem several hundred years before Christ, she would have known "what's in a name." Meaning, character, essence, and personality are in a name. Now if these observations are true of human names, how much more true must they be of the name of God. As Eichrodt (Walter Eichrodt, *Theology of the Old Testament*, trans. by J. A. Baker, 2 Vols., I, 178.) has written,

If the saying *nomina sunt realia* is valid in any

context, it is surely that of the divine name in the ancient world. The question, therefore, of what kind of name the God of Israel bore is no idle one, but can be the means of arriving at an important insight to Israel's religious thought.

The special covenant name of the Israelite national God, the name which he, so to speak, subscribed to the character of the Sinai covenant, is essentially Yahweh.

Here we encounter an incredible paradox. It is self-evident that the name of God must be the most important name in all of Scripture. Surely it is also patent that his name should be known, adored, used, and understood by all who are related to him. Yet, through an almost unbelievable quirk in history, the name of God remains relatively unknown to the Christian public. Jewish people avoided pronouncing God's name due to superstition and a distorted emphasis on one of the Ten Words or Commandments. Early in the Reformation period one Galatinus, a Hebrew scholar, misunderstood the Jewish protective device guarding against saying the name of God when reading the text of Scripture. The result of his confusion is the term "Jehovah."

Hebrew in the Old Testament period was written without vowels. That is, the Hebrew alphabet consisted solely of consonants. When Hebrew became less a living language, Jewish people found it more difficult to pronounce the words in the text without the notation of vowels. So it was that a system of vowel indicators was developed by the Massoretic scholars to aid the reader in pronunciation. It had become the custom of Jewish readers to pronounce the word *Adonai*, which means "lord," whenever the text had the name of God. To insure that this practice continued, the Massoretic scholars inserted the vowels of the word *Adonai* into the consonants of the name of God (YHWH). In this way it was believed that there was a hedge against saying the ineffable name. Galatinus, in about A.D. 1520, misunderstood this "guard," and thought that the vowels were part of the name of God. Hence, by fusing the vowels of one word with the consonants of another, Galatinus gave the church the word "Jehovah," a hybrid term that is not really a Hebrew word at all, and hence a word without real meaning.

The paradox is complete. God has a name. This name is Yahweh. A mispronunciation of that name (Jehovah) is known by many people and is found in our hymns and occasionally in our Bibles. But the name that is known is not really a meaningful Hebrew term. On the other hand, the genuine name of God, Yahweh, is so unknown by the Christian laity that one prominent Bible translation editorialized its explanation for not printing Yahweh in the text (although it is found at times in the margin):

> It is felt by many who are in touch with the laity of our churches that this name Yahweh conveys no religious or spiritual overtones. It is strange, uncommon, and without religious and devotional background. No amount of

scholarly debate can overcome this deficiency. Hence, it was decided to avoid the use of the name in the translation proper (*The New American Standard Bible*, Preface, p. ix).

Yet the emphasis of Scripture is that God has a name and his name has great meaning. We cannot condone the superstition of Israel nor the neglect of the church in this vital issue. It is time, high time, that pious believers begin to exult in the name of the only true God. As Hosea stated with authority, "Even Yahweh, the God of Hosts; Yahweh is his name" (Hosea 12:5).

To regain the "religious or spiritual overtones," felt lacking in the name Yahweh by an editor of the NASB, we need go back to the central text in which God's name was revealed, Exodus 2:23—3:15. Whereas the name of God, Yahweh, was used by believers during the time period of the events of the Book of Genesis, it was not until he was forming his community Israel in Egypt that God "made known" the meaning of his great name. What follows is a brief exposition of one of the most crucial texts in the Old Testament revelation, Exodus 2:23—3:15.

The Exordium (Exodus 2:23-25)

The chapter division between Exodus 2 and 3 seems poorly placed, as Exodus 2:23-25 serves as the introduction to the revelation of the divine name. In these verses we are introduced to the immediate cause for the revelation of God's name:

the extreme distress of his people. In their appeal
and in his response we have the stage set for the
meaning of his name.

The Appeal of the Oppressed People to Their God
(vv. 23-24a)

The section begins with the chronological notice
of the death of the pharaoh. This is significant
background information, for Moses had mur-
dered an Egyptian taskmaster and had then fled
for his life as a fugitive. With the death of the
pharaoh under whom Moses had become a fugitive, the way is prepared for Moses' eventual return to his people in Egypt. But the rest of the
verse emphasizes the conditions among the people
of Israel in their Egyptian bondage. A Hebrew
stylistic device, the use of varied synonyms in
compressed speech, is employed that heightens
the emotional tone of the verse to a fever pitch.
The text (verses 23-24a) reads:

> Now it came about in the course of those
> many days that the king of Egypt died.
>> And the sons of Israel *sighed* because of the
>> bondage,
>> and they *cried out*;
>> and their *cry for help* because of their bon-
>> dage rose up to God.
> So God heard their *groaning*.

Four terms are used to express the intensity of
the oppression of God's people. These words,
"sighed," "cried out," "cry for help," and "groan-

ing" work with each other, reverberating in quadraphonic sound to give, in brief space, an overwhelming impression of the terrible suffering of Israel. Four different Hebrew words are used by Torah to help us "feel" their pain. Now, it is no surprise that slaves in oppression scream to God. The surprise is that God responds. In his response, we learn something universally true about him and we are prepared for the meaning of his name.

The Answer of God to His Oppressed People (vv. 24-25)

These words read:

> So God *heard* their groaning;
> And God *remembered* his covenant with
>   Abraham, Isaac and Jacob.
> And God *saw* the sons of Israel,
> And God *took notice* of them.

As if in direct response to the four terms for Israel's distress, there are four verbs used of God's responding actions. These verbs are characteristic of his nature. There is a sense in which it may be said that when the people of God suffer, he is not left unaffected by their pain. He hears, he remembers, he sees, and he takes notice. The last verb of the four is rendered "took notice" in the text of the NASB. The AV had rendered the verb "had respect." Actually the margin of the NASB and the text of the *New Scofield Reference Bible* translate the original more accurately by reading "God knew." This important verb *know* is the climax of the section. God was experientially and intimately involved in the suffering of his people. He hears, he remembers, he sees, and he knows. These verbs, as in the case of the words for Israel's distress, work together in a similar quadraphonic nature to give the impassioned response of God. It is not simply that he is aware of his people's needs or that he is passively observing. Rather, he knows! In these verbs there is also the latent promise that he will do something about their need. And he does indeed do so in the revelation of his name in chapter three.

The Theophany at the Burning Bush (Exodus 3:1-12)

Few chapters in the Old Testament are as crucial for our understanding of the nature of God as is this one. Exodus chapter three ranks in importance in the Old Testament as does John chapter three in the New Testament. For it is in this chapter that God reveals the meaning of his great name Yahweh. The setting is the well-known account of the theophany at the burning bush. On occasion one gets the impression that theophanies, the appearances of God to man, were a somewhat regular phenomenon in the Old Testament period. Such is not the case. Every theophany is a marvel of his condescending grace. Imagine! God revealing something of his glory to man! In this occasion there had been no word from God for over four hundred years as Israel was in Egyptian bondage. And now he appears to a shepherd on the backside of the desert. There is some humor to the passage. Not a lot happens in the desert; very little is new in the life of a shepherd. All at once, Moses, who has been in the desert for forty years, sees something genuinely new: a bush burning without diminishing. His words, "I must turn aside now, and see this marvelous sight, why the bush is not burned up" (v. 3), are words of authentic wonder.

An Amplification of God's Answer to His Oppressed People

When Moses approached the bush he was told to remove his sandals, for the ground on which he was standing was holy, set apart, made different because of the appearance of the shadow of God's glory. In the conversation between God and Moses (imagine that—a conversation with the God of glory!), there is an amplification of the answer God gave his people in chapter two. For the four verbs which we noted in verses 24 and 25 are used again in these verses to bring even more emphasis on their importance. These verbs—God hears, God remembers, God sees, God knows—are indicative of the nature of God. Although he is described in some texts as residing in incomparable glory—lofty, high, and exalted—yet he stoops to meet the needs of his people. Psalm 113:4-6 vividly describes this blending of God's transcendence and his relatedness to his creation.

In these verses of Exodus chapter three we are reminded again of God's characteristic relatedness to his people in the concepts of hearing, remembering, seeing, and knowing. The verb "to "to hear" is found in verse 7 in the translation, "I have given heed to their cry because of their taskmasters." It is found again in verse 9 in the words, "The cry of the sons of Israel has come to me" (cf. 2:23). We should emphasize that God is not saying simply that the sounds were heard, but rather that he hears with compassion and with readiness to deliver.

The word "remember" is not used in chapter three, but the concept is clearly stated in verse 6 in the words,

> I am the God of your father,
> and the God of Abraham,
> the God of Isaac,
> and the God of Jacob.

Whenever we have this litany, God of the three patriarchs, the theological assertion is that God *remembers* his covenant with the fathers. Compare again Exodus 2:24, "and God remembered his covenant with Abraham, Isaac, and Jacob." The same terminology is found in Exodus 3:15, below.

The verb "to see," with God as subject, is found twice. In 3:7 we read, "I have surely seen the affliction of my people who are in Egypt." The rendering "surely seen" reflects the emphatic Hebrew original wherein two forms of the Hebrew root "to see" are employed. Again, verse 9 reads, "I have seen the oppression with which the Egyptians are oppressing them." As in the other relationship verbs, it is not sufficient to say that God was "aware" of the plight of his people. The denotation of the verb "see," with God as subject, in this context is "to see with compassion and with anticipated action."

The fourth verb of relationship used in chapter two (to reappear in chapter three) is the significant term "to know." This is found in verse 7 in the words, "for I am aware of their sufferings." As in the case of the verb "to know" in 2:25, it seems that the NASB is somewhat weak in the reading "to be aware." The AV seems stronger in its reading, "for I *know* their sorrows." That is, as is indicated by the other verbs, there is some sense in which God participates, he experiences, he *knows* the sufferings of his people.

An Addition to God's Answer
to His Oppressed People

Having reiterated the four verbs of relationship, the text of Exodus three now takes us to something new. In addition to these verbs of ongoing relatedness of God to his people, Torah now adds two new verbs that are stunning in their impact: (1) he comes down to deliver, and (2) he promises to be with his own. In these verbs, as we will see, we have the heart of the gospel in the Old Testament. In terms of the forward-directedness of revelation to the person of Jesus Christ, these two verbs in this context are of the utmost importance.

Exodus 3:8 reads,

> *So I have come down*
> *to deliver them* from the power of the
> Egyptians,

> *and to bring them up* from that land
>> to a good and spacious land,
>> to a land flowing with milk
>> and honey,
>> to the place of the Canaanite and
>> the Hittite and the Amorite and
>> the Perizzite and the Hivite
>> and the Jebusite.

These words are the Old Testament expression of the same activity of God that culminates in the Incarnation. It is God *coming down* to deliver his people from their bondage and to bring them into freedom. There is no clearer expression of the gospel possible in the Old Testament than this text. For this reason the Exodus of Israel from Egypt stands in the same relationship of the New Testament revelation. A believer in the Old Testament was saved not only because he looked forward to the fulfillment of the promises of Jesus Christ, but because he believed in the redemption already accomplished by God when he brought Israel from Egypt. And this act was part of the revelation of his name! Exodus 3:8 is a fundamental text of Old Testament theology. God bursts forth in the human arena to meet their need for deliverance. This is one of the great anticipatory acts of the deliverance wrought in the person of the Lord Jesus Christ.

The second "new" verb in this unit is to be found in verse 12:

> And he said,
>> Certainly *I will be with you,*
>> and this shall be the sign to you that it is I

who have sent you: when you have brought the people out of Egypt, you shall worship God at this mountain.

These words, addressed to Moses, may be regarded as another necessary ingredient in the multiplex meaning of the name of God. His promise *to be with* his own extends the importance of his "coming down." This too is one of the incredible foreshadowings of the gospel in Christ, for he too promises to be with his own.

When the four verbs of relationship—God hears, God remembers, God sees, God knows—are coupled to these two new verbs of God's condescending actions—God comes down, and God will be with you—then the stage is fully set for the revelation of the divine name Yahweh.

The Revelation of the Divine Name Yahweh (Exodus 3:13-15)

The Question of Moses (Exodus 3:13)

Moses, understandably, is hesitant to return to his people in Egypt with the promise of deliverance from slavery and freedom from bondage unless he is most fully assured of his source of authority. He himself had spent a generation in the wilderness as a herdsman because he was an exile and a fugitive from the land of his birth. The people of Israel would be reluctant to accept such startling words from one with so blemished a past. So Moses asks God the fundamental question of theology, "Now they may say to me, 'What is his name?' What shall I say to them?" From all that has been presented earlier in this chapter, it is patently clear that Moses' question was most serious and important. He was asking for the revelation of the essence, character, and meaning of the person of God to be found in his name.

The Response of God (Exodus 3:14, 15)

The response of God to Moses' question is twofold. In verse 14 we read:

> And God said to Moses,
> "I AM WHO I AM";
> and he said,
> "Thus you shall say to the sons of Israel,
> 'I AM has sent me to you.'"

This is the first part of the twofold response of God. One scholar has puzzled over these words and has remarked that Moses asked a good question only to have God respond with a riddle. But if we look closely enough, we see that this is a most marvelous answer.

In the words I AM, which most versions rightly put in capitals as something very special, God asserts in the strongest means possible in human language his absolute being. He exists dependent upon nothing or no one excepting his own will. "I AM!" No one can say those words in the sense of Exodus 3:14 excepting God himself. The Creator of the universe is the only personality who does not depend upon the universe for his existence.

We must insist, however, that the words I AM refer not to static being but to *active* existence. All of the biblical descriptions of the glory of God are dynamic in nature. Never is God immobile, passive, static—rather he is charged with his own life, power, and dynamic. When God says of himself, "I AM," he speaks of his active existence, pulsing with power and throbbing with life.

The second part of God's response to Moses is in the next verse:

> And God, furthermore, said to Moses,
> "Thus you shall say to the sons of Israel,
> 'YAHWEH
> The God of your fathers
> The God of Abraham
> The God of Isaac
> · and the God of Jacob
> has sent me to you.'
> This is my Name forever,
> And this is my Memorial-Name to all generations."

The text is indented so that the grammatical relationships are more readily apparent. "Yahweh" is the subject of the verb "has sent," and is the term considered in the last two lines, "This is my Name forever, and this is my Memorial-Name to all generations." In the leading English versions, of course, the word rendered above as "Yahweh" is translated as "LORD."

First, we may make an observation concerning the relationship of the two terms, "I AM" (v. 14) and "Yahweh" (v. 15). While these seem to be remote from each other, they are really closely related. Both terms are forms of the Hebrew verb "to be." The English translation of the Hebrew word in verse 14 (*'ehyeh*) as "I AM," reflects the fact that this verb is a first-person form of the root. The word "Yahweh" is merely the transliteration of the third person of the same verb. Hence, Yahweh means "HE IS." Whereas in Exodus 3:14 God says of himself, "I AM," when we speak of him we do not say "I AM," but rather "HE IS." It is for that reason that the third person form of the verb, namely Yahweh, has come down through history as the *Name* of God, as stated clearly in verse 15.

Second, we may now develop a bit further the meaning of Yahweh from that given above. Whereas the words "I AM/HE IS" are appropriate renderings of the respective Hebrew verbs in these two verses, they are not the only renderings possible. Equally possible is the future tense: "I WILL BE/HE WILL BE." In fact, this is precisely the translation given of the Hebrew word *'ehyeh* in verse 12, "Certainly *I will be* with you." The close association of the content of verse 12 to verses 14-15 must have some influence. The terms "I AM/Yahweh" speak not only of God's absolute existence, as noted above, but also of *his relatedness to his own people*. Many Old Testament scholars like to speak of "Yahweh" as the "covenant name" of God. They are correct. In this name, he relates himself to his people forever. He says of himself, 'I AM"; he also says of himself, "I will be with you." Hence, his existence, in a dynamic and powerful expression, is related to our good! This is the wonder of *his name*.

Is there any wonder, then, that the name of God is the most blessed vocable of human speech? Is there any question of its merit? Any reason for our reluctance to use it? God says of his name Yahweh that this is his name forever, and that this is his Memorial-designation for all generations. By his name he posits his being. Further, by his name he declares he will continue to exist for our good. In this one word we have blended together in perfect unity God's transcendence and his relatedness to his people. "Blessed be the Name, Yahweh, forever!"

The Relationship of Yahweh to Jesus

One item is left for mention, and that is the relationship of the name "Jesus" to the name "Yahweh." Three notes may be given briefly.

Firstly, the name "Jesus" is explained to the reader in the words of the angel to Joseph, "You shall call his name Jesus, for it is he who will save his people from their sins" (Matthew 1:21). These words explain that the meaning of the name of Jesus is drawn from its Hebrew elements. The name "Jesus" is a compound term of the name of God, Yahweh, and the Hebrew verb "to save." Jesus' name, then, is an explanation of Exodus 3:8, "I have come down to deliver them." In the person of Jesus we see Yahweh in the ultimate condescension, coming down in the final act of redemption, the goal of the forward-directedness of revelation of Exodus 3:8.

Second, on more than one occasion Jesus' authority was challenged by his listeners. One of the most dramatic confrontations is found in John 8, where Jesus is even accused of being demon possessed (v. 52). The Jewish enemies of their Jewish Messiah pressed him to compare himself with the father of all Jews, Abraham himself. Jesus' response can never be forgotten:

> Truly, truly, I say to you,
>> before Abraham was born, I AM
>>> (John 8:58).

The NASB has rightly rendered the last word in capitals, for here we have the unequivocal attestation by Christ of his deity. When Jesus said of himself, "I AM," his Jewish listeners took up stones to put him to death for the grossest form of blasphemy, the use of the divine name of himself. Never let anyone tell you that Jesus did not claim to be very God. In terms that every Jew understood immediately, Jesus called himself the same words that God used in Exodus 3:14. As was stated above, whereas God says of himself, "I AM," we say of him, "HE IS."

Finally, the last explication of the divine name in the person of Jesus Christ is to be found in his words to his disciples on the occasion of his ascension to heaven. In the closing of the Great Commission, Jesus promises his own, "Lo, I am with you always, even to the end of the age" (Matthew 28:20). Again, this relates to the revelation of the divine name in Exodus 3. More specifically, this verse in Matthew relates to verse 12, "Certainly I will be with you."

In the name Jesus we have the final explication of the name YAHWEH. Hence, he has "the name which is above every name" (Philippians 2:9). In his life and death, Jesus explained to his followers the meaning of the name of God. He was able to declare this as fact in his high priestly prayer in these words: "I manifested thy name to the men whom thou gavest me out of the world" (John 17:6).

"What's in a name?" If the name is the name of God—*everything* is in that name; life, reality, and relationship to the living God!

Truly, Yahweh is the *name* that surrounds his glory!